THE REVISED VERSION
EDITED FOR THE USE OF SCHOOLS

THE BOOK OF JOSHUA

T0381942

THE BOOK OF JOSHUA

EDITED BY

THE REV. P. J. BOYER, M.A.
VICAR OF ROTHERSTHORPE, NORTHAMPTON

CAMBRIDGE
AT THE UNIVERSITY PRESS
1911

CAMBRIDGE
UNIVERSITY PRESS

University Printing House, Cambridge CB2 8BS, United Kingdom

Published in the United States of America by Cambridge University Press, New York

Cambridge University Press is part of the University of Cambridge.

It furthers the University's mission by disseminating knowledge in the pursuit of education, learning and research at the highest international levels of excellence.

www.cambridge.org
Information on this title: www.cambridge.org/9781107650954

First published 1911
First paperback edition 2014

A catalogue record for this publication is available from the British Library

ISBN 978-1-107-65095-4 Paperback

PREFACE BY THE GENERAL EDITOR
FOR THE OLD TESTAMENT

THE aim of this series of commentaries is to explain the Revised Version for young students, and at the same time to present, in a simple form, the main results of the best scholarship of the day.

The General Editor has confined himself to supervision and suggestion. The writer is, in each case, responsible for the opinions expressed and for the treatment of particular passages.

A. H. MᶜNEILE.

January, 1910.

CONTENTS

Available for download in colour from www.cambridge.org/9781107650954

INTRODUCTION.

I. THE BOOK, AND THE HERO.

(i) THE Book of Joshua is so called, not because it was written by Joshua but because it deals with the history of Israel under his leadership. It describes the events between the death of Moses and the death of Joshua[1], and thus forms a fitting conclusion to the early history of Israel as given in the Pentateuch. The people chosen by God are left in peaceful and secure possession of the land that God had promised them. A definite stage in their history has been reached.

This connexion between *Joshua* and the Pentateuch, demanded by the history, is confirmed by the fact that in the book of Joshua, but not beyond, the same literary documents can be traced as in the Pentateuch. This shows that their authors intended to include in their narrative the occupation of Canaan by Israel; and the cutting short of the narrative at the death of Moses (Dt. xxxiv.) and the omission of the grand *finale* do them an injustice. In recent times the word *Hexateuch* (i.e. the six-fold volume) has been coined for the purpose of emphasizing the fact that *Joshua* belongs both historically and critically to the Pentateuch.

[1] The first portion of the book (chs. i.–xii.) relates to the conquest of Canaan, which is represented as the result of orderly and progressive movements, (*a*) the passage of the Jordan and entrance to Canaan (i.–v. 12), (*b*) the capture of Jericho and Ai, and eventually of the whole of the southern part of the land (v. 13–x. 43), (*c*) a decisive campaign in the N. (xi.). This portion is closed by a list of the conquered kings, both E. and W. of Jordan (xii.).

The second portion deals with the division of the conquered land (xiii.–xxi.). Some appendices are added, relating (xxii.) the dismissal of the trans-Jordanic tribes and the erection of an altar by them, and (xxiii., xxiv.) two farewell speeches of Joshua and final notices.

(ii) On reading the book of Joshua one cannot but notice its Deuteronomic setting. Passages breathing the spirit of Deuteronomy begin the book and close it, and are found interspersed throughout it, more especially in chapters i.-xii. It is clear, therefore, that the book has passed through the hands of Deuteronomists. Indeed, it might be said that they made the book ; for they took stories which related to the conquest of Canaan, and which formed part of an old history book[1] that dealt with events from the creation of the world to the occupation of the land, and made of them a narrative of their own, marked by the tone and colour of their earnest beliefs. They reset these gems of popular tradition.

As far as can be seen, when the book left the hands of the Deuteronomists it contained little more than the first twelve chapters[2], and chapter xxiii.[3] The allotment of the conquered land does not seem to have interested the Deuteronomists ; with them the all-important matter was the conquest. Later writers, however, supplied this deficiency, and to the Priestly School, which flourished about 100 years after the destruction of Jerusalem by the Chaldeans, we owe the full details of tribal inheritances that occupy the larger portion of chapters xiii. to xxi.

(iii) Who were the Deuteronomists ? They were sturdy adherents of the teaching and principles of Deuteronomy, who formed a very prominent school of thought in the last century of the existence of the kingdom of Judah. They believed that God ruled the world, and that God loved Israel ; the story of Israel was, therefore, the story of God's dealing with the people of his choice. They read the story of the conquest of Canaan in the light of this

---

[1] Commonly designated JE, as being the product of the union of two older works, J, a Judaean document, and E, a north-Israelite document.

[2] A few verses in these chapters belong to the late Priestly writer :—iii. 4a, iv. 15-17, 19, v. 10-12, vii. 1, ix. 15b, 17-21.

[3] Ch. xxiv., though belonging to the old history book, was not admitted by the Deuteronomists, probably because it did not agree with their own version in ch. xxiii. (cf. on xxiii. 8).

belief; and they held that as God had chosen Israel and promised them Canaan, the conquest of Canaan, after the punishing severities of the wilderness, could not have been unduly delayed. It must have been God's purpose that his people should make a speedy and triumphant entrance into their heritage, and that their conquest should be complete. The hostile kings who opposed Israel in their God-given task must be treated with merciless rigour; the people must be exterminated[1].

The story of the conquest of Canaan, as told by the Deuteronomic writers, is intended to show the irresistible power of Israel under the guidance of God. After reading it the mental picture we retain is that of a victorious entry into Canaan, made at one time, by a united people, under one leader, Joshua, after a short and sharp struggle which was marked by no disaster, for the repulse at Ai (ch. vii.) does not deserve this name.

This picture, it will be seen presently, is very different from that which, dimly outlined in the book of Joshua itself, stands clearly revealed by the excavations in Canaan. And in endeavouring to account for the discrepancy we have to assume that the Deuteronomists, as they glanced back over the centuries which had elapsed since the events they were recording took place, intended to represent as speedy and complete the process which placed Israel in secure possession of Canaan, to compress the work of many generations into the span of a few brief years, and to focus the reader's attention less on wearisome and disjointed details than on the splendid result.

By adopting this method of interpreting the march of events they took, as it were, a short cut to their destination, but they destroyed the true historical perspective.

---

[1] Cf. the Deuteronomic summaries in x. 40–43, xi. 16–20, and xxi. 43–45.

Their finished picture, therefore, can only be considered ideal.

The grounds for this statement are as follows :—

1. *It is highly improbable that the Canaanites should have been exterminated in a few years.* They were well provided with weapons of defence ; many of their cities were fortresses (x. 20) ; and as they were fighting for hearth and home they would make a determined stand.

2. *Passages in* Joshua *show that they were not so exterminated*[1].

"The mountain districts of Ephraim and Judah were the first to give way ; in the valleys and lowlands the Canaanites were able to use their "chariots of iron" with effect. Thus it came about that in some parts Israel was in possession, and in others the Canaanites ; and the treaty of Joshua with the Gibeonites (ix. 3–15) shows how the two contestant parties were constrained to recognise each other's independence. The path, therefore, lay open for mutual intercourse and eventually inter-marriage[2]." Even in the days of Solomon (1 K. ix. 20, 21) the Canaanites had not finally disappeared.

3. *The excavations confirm this gradual and partial subjugation of the land.*

They show that the Canaanite civilization and religion glided almost imperceptibly into the civilization and religion of Israel ; there is no trace of the one being forcibly superseded by the other (see section below, on Canaan).

(iv) What, then, is the position of Joshua himself? If the view that dominates the book of Joshua and represents the tribes of Israel as making a united attack on Canaan and fighting side by side till the land was completely subdued, is not justified, the place that is assigned to Joshua as leader of the combined Israelite hosts will require some modification. If, however, the conquest resolved itself into a number of attacks, directed generally by independent bodies of Israelite warriors, now at one spot, now at another, now at one time, now at another, we may well

[1] See xiii. 13, xv. 63, xvi. 10, xvii. 11–13, 16. These passages are extracts from an old account of the conquest, which has been preserved more fully, but by no means completely, in the first chapter of *Judges.*

[2] Boyer, *Critical and Historical Notes* (1908), p. 427.

believe that Joshua headed one or more of these, though his name does not occur as a leader in the accounts of the attacks described in *Judges* i.

It is remarkable, too, that if Joshua had performed the mighty deeds ascribed to him in the book that bears his name, later generations of his countrymen should have so completely ignored his claim to grateful recognition ; for outside the Hexateuch he is mentioned only in Jud. i. 1 (a late editorial note), ii. 6–9 (=Josh. xxiv. 28–30), ii. 21, 23 (Deuteronomic) ; 1 Kings xvi. 34 (his curse) ; 1 Chron. vii. 27 (a list of names), and Neh. viii. 17 (a notice about the Feast of Tabernacles). No writer of any kind refers to him as a source of inspiration and encouragement until his namesake, Jesus, the son of Sirach, in the second century B.C. includes him in his praise of famous men (Ecclus. xlvi. 1–8).

II. THE LAND, AND ITS STORY.

On account of the belief entertained by the Hebrews themselves (Gen. x. 21) that they were descendants of Shem, the branch of the human family to which they belonged has in modern times been called *Semitic*. The branch, which had its home in Arabia, was a large one, and included many peoples who spoke a radically similar language : Arabians, Aramaeans, Assyrians, Babylonians, Canaanites, Hebrews (and the closely related Ammonites, Edomites, and Moabites), Phoenicians, and others.

The traditional view of the history of the Hebrews has undergone serious modification during the last fifty years, owing to the fact that their own history, and the history of the peoples who were descended from the same stock or with whom they had to do, have become more perfectly known to us through excavation and scientific research. Babylonia, Egypt, Assyria have come to life again at the touch of the explorer's spade. The work of exploration is still being carried on and discoveries are still being made, but at the present time interest may be said to be leaving the valleys of the Euphrates and the Nile in favour of Canaan, N. Syria, and Asia Minor.

(i) The land of Canaan[1] was known to the kings of Babylonia and brought under the influence of Babylonian civilization from a very early period. But after the downfall of the First (Semitic) Dynasty of Babylon, the best known member of which was Ḥammurābi (c. B.C. 2000), the political influence of Babylonia in Western Asia ceased.

(ii) The kings of Egypt obtained a footing in Canaan as early probably as B.C. 3000. It was not, however, till some 1500 years later that Egypt exercised definite sway in the country and ruled it as a Province.

She had just thrown off the foreign yoke of the Hyksos and established herself under a new Dynasty (the XVIIIth, B.C. 1580–1330), some of the kings of which were brilliant warriors. Under the rule of Thutmōsis III (B.C. 1503–1449) she reached the zenith of her power and claimed sovereignty over the larger part of W. Asia, as far, indeed, as the Euphrates. This energetic king made several campaigns in Syria. A list of about 120 Canaanite cities which he reduced was inscribed on the walls of a Temple at Karnak; and among the names are some of those mentioned in *Joshua* :—Beeroth (ix. 17), Beth-anath (xix. 38), Chinneroth (xi. 2), Edrei (xii. 4), Hazor (xi. i), Megiddo and Taanach (xii. 21).

Under Amenhotep IV (B.C. 1383–1365), the last king of any note in Dynasty XVIII., the power of Egypt in western Asia was, as the Amarna Letters show (see below), fast waning, and at the close of the Dynasty Syria was practically lost to her, though in theory she still claimed the overlordship, and indeed asserted her claim with some success under the next Dynasty (1330–1202).

---

[1] The meaning of the word is not known; some think it = "the Lowland." On the name *Palestine* see on xiii. 2.

Seti I (Dynasty XIX) advanced as far as Kadesh on the Orontes, where he fought a battle with some allies of the Hittites (on whom see below). This proved to be the prelude to a lengthy struggle between Hittites and Egyptians, which was not composed till Ramses II (1300–1234), son and successor of Seti I, had been on the throne for 20 years. An agreement was then made between the contending parties, under which the southern portion of the country was secured from disturbance on the part of the Hittites, but it is very questionable whether it accorded complete recognition to the claims of the sovereign power of Egypt.

Meneptah, the son of Ramses II, was obliged to enforce his claim by arms, and among the peoples of Palestine whose subjection he records were the Israelites. If, as is often supposed[1], the Exodus took place in the early part of his reign (c. B.C. 1230)[2], these Israelites must have been a branch of the people which, not having been in Egypt, had gained early possession of a portion of Canaan.

No other king in Dynasty XIX. seems to have exercised any authority in Palestine ; but we know that Ramses III (Dynasty XX), who reigned B.C 1180–1148, made a triumphal march through Syria, and took back with him much spoil.

With this king closes the period of Egyptian history, so far as it can be said to synchronize with that of Israel as recorded in the book of Joshua[3]. Henceforward, the kingdom of Assyria had to be reckoned with as the dominant power of Western Asia. She had already, under Tiglath-pileser I (c. B.C. 1100), pushed her armies across the Euphrates and had entered northern Syria ; and Egypt had no mind to try conclusions with her.

(iii) Canaan was also brought into contact with a power-

---

[1] On the strength of Ex. ii. 23, iv. 19. See McNeile, *Exodus*, p. 13.

[2] So Driver, *Additions and corrections* (to the Book of Genesis), 1909, p. iii.

[3] The date for the entrance of Israel into Canaan cannot fall later than the beginning of the 12th cent. B.C.

ful neighbour in the north—the so-called " Hittites," who are mentioned in the cuneiform inscriptions as "men of the land of Ḥatti," and in Egyptian inscriptions as Ḥeta. Their country lay in the eastern portion of Asia Minor, and the capital was called Ḥatti (the present Boghaz-keui, midway between Angora and Sivas).

Till quite recently very little was known of these Hittites, and our only sources of information were the inscriptions of Babylonia-Assyria, and of Egypt, and the occasional notices in the Old Testament. However, the research and excavation which have done so much in other fields are at length supplying us with first-hand knowledge[1].

In the Amarna Letters the Hittites appear as a constant menace to Egypt from the north, and for the best part of the 14th and 13th centuries, when they were at the height of their power, they proved themselves a match for her, the struggle being ended, as we have seen, by an agreement. The fact that the Hittite monarch, Ḥattusil, himself drew up this agreement shows that the final advantage rested with the Hittites.

(iv) Who the natives of Canaan were in the days of the early Babylonian kings we do not know, but it is probable that they were of a Semitic stock; for Arabia, the home of the Semites, threw off from time to time its surplus population into the adjoining countries, giving a Semitic king (Sargon) to Accad and a Semitic Dynasty to Babylon.

Canaan, therefore, was probably more than once recruited by fresh layers of population from the steppes of Arabia ; and from this quarter it seems probable that the Ḥabiru came, who in the 15th century were seeking a settled home in Canaan or on its border-land. In the present state of our information it is impossible to say exactly who these Ḥabiru were ; but it is difficult to withhold assent from the belief that they included the

---

[1] *The Land of the Hittites* (1910), by Garstang, is the most recent book on the subject. Much information in a concise form will be found in *Ashmolean Museum: Summary Guide* (1910), pp. 68–73.

Hebrews, and perhaps the related peoples, the Moabites, Ammonites, and Edomites[1].

Our knowledge of the Ḥabiru is derived almost entirely from the Amarna Letters[2], a series of despatches belonging to the time of Amenhotep III and IV (c. B.C. 1400), which give a valuable picture of the conditions prevailing in Canaan at that period. Egypt, we find, still retained nominal suzerainty ; but those of the governors or petty princes in Palestine who sought to remain loyal to her were hard put to it to defend themselves and uphold the interests of their overlord. There was, moreover, no political cohesion amongst them, and in most cases they ruled no further than the reach of their sword, a limit which meant the walls of their town and the adjoining land.

The danger to Canaan at this time was two-fold. Within, there was a nationalist party led by the chiefs Abdi-Ashirta and Aziru, and others less prominent. It received much support from the nomads from outside, amongst whom were the Ḥabiru, found only in the neighbourhood of Jerusalem, and the Sutu, who, though ready to place themselves at the disposal of the highest bidder, seem to have allied themselves with the disloyal Canaanites. The whole confederacy was called the Ḥabbatu (i.e. the robbers). This serious state of internal disaffection was aggravated by the pressure of the. Hittites advancing from the north, and resulted in the complete disorganization of all imperial authority[3].

[1] The inclusion of the Hebrews in the Ḥabiru does not necessarily imply that the two names are identical, though this is possible.

[2] Clay tablets inscribed (with but few exceptions) in Babylonian cuneiform, discovered in 1887 at Tell el-Amarna in Egypt. With the exception of seven, which are apparently copies of despatches sent from the Egyptian Court, all the Letters are addressed to Egypt. Some were sent by kings, e.g. of Assyria, Babylon, the Mitanni (a powerful branch of the Hittites, established in northern Mesopotamia), or by other foreign correspondents; but by far the largest portion came from governors of towns in Syria who had received their appointment from the kings of Egypt.

[3] The latest survey of Canaan at this period is by Dhorme in *Revue Biblique* (Oct. 1908, Jan. and July 1909).

The close of the period covered by the Amarna Letters was marked by general political weakness throughout western Asia. No single state was capable of assuming or retaining the chief control. Since the downfall of her first Dynasty Babylon had lost touch with "the Country of the West"; Assyria was only beginning to feel her strength; the Hittites were as yet neither strong nor united enough to become a dominant people; while Egypt, never a great military power, was unable, owing to domestic dissensions, to do more than make promises, or attempt to redeem them by putting forth an occasional effort in defence of territory which she claimed but could not rule.

During this period of confusion the impotence of the great nations became the opportunity of the nomads, who, restless and alert, found they could push their way to places which under a stable government would have been stoutly barred against them. Time and conditions were favourable to a nomad success in Canaan.

(v) The fact revealed by the Amarna Letters, that Canaanite petty princes, and even Egyptian governors resident in Palestine, used Babylonian script for official correspondence[1] with the Pharaoh, shows that Babylon, though bereft of her political ascendency in Canaan at the beginning of the second millennium, had left behind her some abiding traces of her civilization. Such traces may also be seen (i) in the names of deities, which are found mostly as parts of place names[2], and (ii) in ideas and legends (e.g. the stories of the Creation and the Deluge) which may have passed into the possession of the pre-Israelite inhabitants of Canaan, and from them into that of Israel.

[1] Its use, too, in private correspondence is proved by cuneiform tablets found at Lachish and Taanach.

[2] E.g. Shamash (sun god) in Beth-shemesh, Sin (moon god) in Desert of Sin, Anath in Beth-anath (xix. 38). Several other Babylonian gods appear in the Amarna Letters as parts of place or personal names (Ninib, Addu = Adad, Nebo).

While, however, admitting some such traces as these it is necessary to remember that there is the probability, less of direct Babylonian influence than of indirect. The culture of Babylon passed through Hittite and N. Syrian lands before it reached Canaan[1], and it is known that the Babylonian cuneiform writing was in use in Ḥatti-land a thousand years before the Amarna period. At the same time our acquaintance with the Hittite civilization is at present so slender that we are not warranted in drawing sure conclusions either on this question or on the more general one of the effect of that civilization on Canaan[2].

(vi) Besides the Babylonian, or (as we may term it) Babylonian-Hittite, influence on Canaan, we have to take account of that exerted by Egypt. It is only natural to expect that the close and constant intercourse between the two countries, existing from at least B.C. 2000, and the relation in which they stood to one another, would lead to the discovery of traces of the highly developed civilization of Egypt.

This expectation has not been belied; for the excavations in Palestine have brought to light Egyptian inscriptions, statues of gods, countless scarabs, pottery, and, in general, many evidences of the worship of the gods of Egypt—Amon, corresponding to the Babylonian sun-god Shamash, being an especial favourite —under whose protection, indeed, the land was placed, as being subject to Egypt.

Here, again, however, a caution must be entered, for there is a danger of exaggerating Egyptian influence. It was by no means inconsiderable; time may prove it to have been even greater than that of Babylon; but it was never strong enough completely to subdue and absorb the native culture[3].

[1] Cf. S. A. Cook, *Expositor* Aug. 1909, pp. 101–103.

[2] In the Amarna Letters Palestinian princes bearing Hittite names are mentioned: e.g. Abdi-ḥiba ("the servant of Ḥiba," a Hittite Goddess) is the name of a Governor of Jerusalem. The Hittites, in general, were an enterprising and warlike people, and Benzinger (*Hebräische Archäologie*[2], p. 51) thinks it probable that they taught the Canaanites a great deal in the working of metals and in the science of war. The Egyptians, as well as the Canaanites, copied the Hittite war-chariots.

[3] Cf. S. A. Cook, *Religion of Ancient Palestine*, pp. 74–80, 111–113.

(vii) The *religion of Canaan* was enabled to hold its own against the influences both of Egypt and Babylonia. Though to a certain extent leavened by the ideas and customs of these countries its native elements can be clearly recognised. Chief among the Canaanite gods stood Baal, who had sanctuaries everywhere. Astarte, the consort of Baal, was almost as popular[1]. Other deities were Zedek (x. i), Gad (xi. 17, xv. 37), and perhaps Zaphon (xiii. 27). Religious rites were performed, not in temples, but in the open, at holy places which were also generally high places[2], that is, places on an eminence. Every holy place had its altar, its stone pillar or pillars, and its wooden post which represented the tree goddess Ashērah and was called by this name (cf. Ex. xxxiv. 13, etc.).

The study of the Canaanite religion, as revealed by the excavations, is important for the understanding of the history of Israel in Canaan. While the Israelites were making themselves masters of the land they were much influenced by it, and they adopted many of its customs, which persisted until late times and were strongly denounced by the Prophets[3]. In fact, for some centuries the religion of the great mass of the people was "a peculiar mixture of the religion of Canaan and that of Jehovah. A really sudden break, therefore, between the Canaanite and Israelite civilizations is not demonstrated by the excavations...but only a gradual passing of the one into the other[4]."

---

[1] Where (as e.g. 1 S. vii. 4) the plural forms *Baalim* and *Ashtaroth* occur, they indicate the local deities. Cf. also *Anathoth* (i.e. the Anaths) in Josh. xxi. 18.

[2] Cf. Driver, *Modern Research as illustrating the Bible*, pp. 60, 61.

[3] See 1 K. xiv. 23, 24; 2 K. xiv. 4, xvi. 4, xviii. 4; Hos. iv. 13; Jer. iii. 6; Dt. vii. 5, xii. 2, 3.

[4] Sellin, *Neue Kirchliche Zeitschrift* (Feb. 1905), p. 129. Cf. S. A. Cook (*Expositor*, *ut supr.* p. 99), "There is no sudden change in the pottery, in the sacred places, or in the forms of culture. Civilisation and religion show no sensible alteration"; and see *Palestine Exploration Fund: Quart. St.* 1904, p. 123;

(viii) From this witness of the excavations, which is decisive on the point that there was no volcanic interruption of the existing Canaanite civilization and religion, it may be inferred that the land was only gradually occupied by Israel. If in the course of a few years (see on xiv. 10) the whole Canaanite civilization had been swept away and replaced by the rude and primitive methods of the victorious nomads, and if a root and branch extermination of the Canaanite peoples had taken place, clear indications of such a "break" would have been discovered by excavation.

The exact duration of the process which ended in the complete mastery of the land by Israel is not known ; but it is certain that it must be reckoned by centuries rather than by years. We know that in the latter part of the 15th century the aggressive movements of the Ḥabiru were in operation, and although some of the raids would be unsuccessful, we may be sure that by B.C. 1350 there would be Ḥabiru settlements firmly rooted in Canaan.

With this agree (i) the appearance of a people named Asher, thought by some to be an Israelite clan, resident in Palestine at the beginning of the xixth Egyptian Dynasty (c. B.C. 1330), and (ii) the mention of "Israel" as resident in Palestine and as having been defeated, which is found on an inscription of Meneptaḥ (B.C. 1234–1214).

Whether any of the Hebrew immigrants who had gained a footing in Canaan before the close of Meneptaḥ's reign belonged to those who had escaped from bondage in Egypt is a question that depends on the date of the Exodus. If the Exodus took place c. B.C. 1230 (see above, p. xiii) the people could not have entered Canaan for at least 40 years afterwards. If, on the other hand, the tradition mentioned in 1 K. vi. 1 is worthy of credence, the Exodus would be a *fait accompli* by B.C. 1400.

1907, p. 203 ; and 1910, pp. 62–64 ; Hugues Vincent, *Canaan d'après l'exploration récente* (1907), p. 204 ; and Kittel, *Die Alttestamentliche Wissenschaft* (1910), III. 3.

But whatever date we assign to the Exodus it seems
necessary to admit that the people who then gained their
freedom, and afterwards survived the wanderings in the
desert, formed only a portion of the later Hebrew population of Canaan. The biblical tradition (Gen. xlvi. 1–6)
tells how this portion came to be connected with Egypt;
but it was of the same stock as the Ḥabiru, and when
settled in possession it made common cause with them.

CHRONOLOGICAL TABLE.

	B.C.
Ḥammurābi (king of Babylon), about ...	2000
Eighteenth Egyptian Dynasty, about ...	1580–1330
Thutmōsis III	1503–1449
Amarna Letters, about	1400
Ḥabiru raids on Palestine, about ...	1400
Amenhotep IV	1383–1365
Nineteenth Egyptian Dynasty, about ...	1330–1202
Ramses II	1300–1234
Agreement between Egypt and the Hittites	1280
Meneptaḥ	1234–1214
Exodus of Israel from Egypt (p. xiii), about	1230
"Israel" resident in Palestine (Men-eptaḥ's stele) (p. xix), about ...	1220
Twentieth Egyptian Dynasty, about ...	1200–1090
Ramses III	1200–1169
(Earliest records of the Philistines in the reign of this monarch.)	
Solomon, about	970
J (p. viii), about	850
E (p. viii), about	750
JE (p. viii), about	650
Deuteronomy, about	621
Priestly writers, about	500

THE BOOK OF JOSHUA

i. 1–9. *God commands Joshua to cross the Jordan and take possession of Canaan, and promises him good success on condition that he keeps all that Moses commanded.*

NOW it came to pass after the death of Moses the **1** servant of the LORD, that the LORD spake unto Joshua the son of Nun, Moses' minister, saying, Moses **2** my servant is dead; now therefore arise, go over this

---

i. 1. Now] And, a rendering which shows more clearly the close connexion between the book of Joshua and the Pentateuch (Introd. p. vii).

the LORD] The printing of this word in small capitals is intended to remind the reader that it is a rendering of *Yahweh*, the proper name of the God of Israel, and to distinguish it from the rendering of the ordinary Hebrew word for "lord" (*ādōn*). Both words occur in iii. 13, "the ark of the LORD, the Lord of all the earth." *Yahweh* means "He who is," that is, the God who lives and is known by his works. Read Dt. xxxii. 39, 1 S. ii. 6–8; and see note on iii. 10. Jehovah (Ex. vi. 2, etc.) is an incorrect reading of Yahweh.

Joshua] He is first mentioned in connexion with the fight at Rephidim (Ex. xvii. 8, 9), and was according to a later tradition (see on xiv. 6) one of the chosen spies. Alone, with Caleb (Jos. xiv. 6–10), he was allowed to survive the desert wanderings (Num. xiii. 8, 16, xiv. 6, 38). The attendant of Moses (Ex. xxiv. 13, xxxiii. 11; cf. Dt. i. 38) he eventually became his successor (Dt. xxxiv. 9). In Num. xiii. 8 (P) his name is given as Hoshea (= "salvation"), and it is stated (*v.* 16) that it was changed by Moses to Jehoshua, or Joshua (= "Jehovah is salvation").

Jordan, thou, and all this people, unto the land which I do
3 give to them, even to the children of Israel. Every place
that the sole of your foot shall tread upon, to you have
4 I given it, as I spake unto Moses. From the wilderness,
and this Lebanon, even unto the great river, the river
Euphrates, all the land of the Hittites, and unto the great
sea toward the going down of the sun, shall be your border.
5 There shall not any man be able to stand before thee all
the days of thy life: as I was with Moses, so I will be with
6 thee : I will not fail thee, nor forsake thee. Be strong and
of a good courage : for thou shalt cause this people to inherit
the land which I sware unto their fathers to give them.
7 Only be strong and very courageous, to observe to do
according to all the law, which Moses my servant commanded thee : turn not from it to the right hand or to
the left, that thou mayest have good success whithersoever

---

4. the wilderness] The wilderness of Paran, of which Zin
(Num. xxxiv. 3) formed a part, lay S. of Canaan. The other
boundaries are probably :—E. (the eastern range of Lebanon,
called Anti-libanus), N. (the upper course of the Euphrates), and
W. (the Mediterranean Sea) ; but they must be considered ideal,
for no part of the Mediterranean coast ever passed into the full
possession of the Israelites, and in the N. they never reached
Hamath (xiii. 5).

and this Lebanon] As no part of Lebanon could have been
visible it has been suggested that **unto Lebanon** should be read.

all the land of the Hittites] These words should probably be
omitted. So LXX ; and cf. Dt. xi. 24. For the Hittites see
Introd. p. xiv.

the great sea] i.e. the Mediterranean (so xv. 12, Num.
xxxiv. 6).

5. There shall not any man etc.] So x. 8, xxi. 44, xxiii. 9.
A Deuteronomic exaggeration. Cf. vii. 4, xiii. 13 etc. and
Introd. p. ix.

I will not fail thee] I will not let thee fall.

6. Be strong and of a good courage] So *vv.* 7, 9. From
x. 24-26 and Dt. xx. 15-18 it will be seen that the "courage"
was to be displayed in the unrelenting destruction of the native
population of Canaan. See note on vi. 17.

7. the law] should probably be omitted, with LXX. The
original Heb. text apparently did not contain the words.

thou goest. This book of the law shall not depart out 8
of thy mouth, but thou shalt meditate therein day and
night, that thou mayest observe to do according to all
that is written therein : for then thou shalt make thy
way prosperous, and then thou shalt have good success.
Have not I commanded thee?   Be strong and of a good 9
courage ; be not affrighted, neither be thou dismayed : for
the LORD thy God is with thee whithersoever thou goest.

10, 11.   *Preparations for the passage of the Jordan.*

Then Joshua commanded the officers of the people, 10
saying, Pass through the midst of the camp, and com- 11
mand the people, saying, Prepare you victuals ; for within
three days ye are to pass over this Jordan, to go in to
possess the land, which the LORD your God giveth you to
possess it.

12–18.   *The trans-Jordanic tribes on being reminded of
their part in the coming struggle promise their hearty co-
operation* (see Num. xxxii.).

And to the Reubenites, and to the Gadites, and to the 12
half tribe of Manasseh, spake Joshua, saying, Remember 13

---

8. With the thought of this verse should be compared Ps. i.
2, 3.
This book of the law] The expressions " this law," " this
book of the law," are frequent in Dt. and in passages, like the
present, which are kindred to Dt.   As Dt. i. 5, iv. 8 show, the
reference is to the law which Moses is represented as expounding
in Dt., and not to the fuller legislation embodied in Ex.-Num.
which was a later growth.   The word rendered "book" means
" writing," and this writing might be on stones (viii. 32).   The
book of later times (Jer. xxxvi. 18) was a roll of parchment or
papyrus leaves attached to a rod.
11. victuals] from the Latin *victus*, ptc. of *vivere* " to live."
More rarely the sing. *victual* is found (Ex. xii. 39, 1 K. iv. 27).
It should be noticed that according to the statement of another
writer in v. 12 the supply of manna had not yet ceased.
within three days] Not, as may be seen from ii. 16, 22, iii. 2,
to be taken literally, but as = " after a short time," " before long."

the word which Moses the servant of the LORD commanded you, saying, The LORD your God giveth you rest,
14 and will give you this land. Your wives, your little ones,
and your cattle, shall abide in the land which Moses gave
you beyond Jordan ; but ye shall pass over before your
brethren armed, all the mighty men of valour, and shall
15 help them ; until the LORD have given your brethren rest,
as *he hath given* you, and they also have possessed the
land which the LORD your God giveth them : then ye
shall return unto the land of your possession, and possess
it, which Moses the servant of the LORD gave you beyond
16 Jordan toward the sunrising. And they answered Joshua,
saying, All that thou hast commanded us we will do, and
17 whithersoever thou sendest us we will go. According as
we hearkened unto Moses in all things, so will we hearken
unto thee : only the LORD thy God be with thee, as he
18 was with Moses. Whosoever he be that shall rebel
against thy commandment, and shall not hearken unto
thy words in all that thou commandest him, he shall be
put to death : only be strong and of a good courage.

ii. 1–7. *The spies, on being sent to Jericho, stay with Rahab*
who hides them and gives false information to the pursuers.

2 And Joshua the son of Nun sent out of Shittim two
men as spies secretly, saying, Go view the land, and

---

14. beyond Jordan] The writer, living on the W. of the
river, means by these words the country E. of the Jordan—**toward
the sunrising** (as he adds in the next verse). This, indeed, is the
usual meaning of **beyond Jordan**; see ii. 10, vii. 7, ix. 10, xiv. 3,
xvii. 5, xxii. 4, xxiv. 8, and with the addition of **eastward** etc.,
xii. 1, xiii. 8, 27, 32, xviii. 7, xx. 8. In four passages, however,
all occurring in the book of Joshua (v. i, ix. 1, xii. 7, xxii. 7),
the phrase is used of the western side.

ii. 1. Shittim] Heb. = "the acacia trees." Shittim has not
been identified for certain, but it is probably the same as Abila
(cf. Num. xxxiii. 49), which has been by some identified with
Kefrēn, about 6 miles east of the Jordan and in a line with
Jericho.

Jericho. And they went, and came into the house of an harlot whose name was Rahab, and lay there. And it 2 was told the king of Jericho, saying, Behold, there came men in hither to-night of the children of Israel to search out the land. And the king of Jericho sent unto Rahab, 3 saying, Bring forth the men that are come to thee, which are entered into thine house : for they be come to search out all the land. And the woman took the two men, and 4 hid them ; and she said, Yea, the men came unto me, but I wist not whence they were : and it came to pass about 5 the time of the shutting of the gate, when it was dark, that the men went out : whither the men went I wot not : pursue after them quickly ; for ye shall overtake them.

Jericho] lay about 5 miles west of the Jordan and about 1 from the hill-country of Judah. In Dt. xxxiv. 3 it is called "the city of palm trees," but these have quite disappeared. After being "devoted" by Joshua (vi. 21-26) it was re-built (xviii. 21, Judg. iii. 13, 2 S. x. 5). The Jericho which our Saviour knew had been restored and beautified by Herod the Great (B.C. 37-4). At the present day excavations, made on the site of the old town, have revealed the amazing strength of the outer wall. Houses have been discovered of three different periods, Canaanite, early Israelite, and later Israelite (c. B.C. 700). Cf. Driver, *Modern Research*, p. 92.

Rahab] Heb. *Raḥab*, quite distinct from *Rahab* (Ps. lxxxvii. 4, Is. li. 9 etc.). With the exception of vi. 17-25 she is not again mentioned in the O.T. In the N.T. she appears as an ancestress of David (Matt. i. 5), and is held up as an example of faith (Heb. xi. 31) and good works (Jas. ii. 25).

2. the king of Jericho] One of the numerous petty kings in Canaan (Introd. p. xv). See the list in xii. 9-24.

to-night] The mention of their departure at nightfall (*v.* 5) is from a different writer.

4. And the woman took the two men, and hid them] This sentence interrupts the conversation and cannot be in its proper place.

wist] so Ex. xvi. 15, Luke ii. 49, is the past tense of *to wit* (A.-S. *witan* = "to know") found in A.V. in Ex. ii. 4, 2 Cor. viii. 1. The present tense is **wot** (as in *v.* 5 and in the A.V. Gen. xxi. 26 etc.). R.V. retains the form *wist* both in the O. and the N.T., but *wot* occurs only here in the O.T.

6 But she had brought them up to the roof, and hid them
with the stalks of flax, which she had laid in order upon
7 the roof. And the men pursued after them the way to
Jordan unto the fords : and as soon as they which pursued
after them were gone out, they shut the gate.

8-11. *Rahab's confession.*

8 And before they were laid down, she came up unto them
9 upon the roof; and she said unto the men, I know that
the LORD hath given you the land, and that your terror is
fallen upon us, and that all the inhabitants of the land
10 melt away before you. For we have heard how the LORD
dried up the water of the Red Sea before you, when ye
came out of Egypt ; and what ye did unto the two kings
of the Amorites, that were beyond Jordan, unto Sihon
11 and to Og, whom ye utterly destroyed. And as soon as
we had heard it, our hearts did melt, neither did there
remain any more spirit in any man, because of you : for
the LORD your God, he is God in heaven above, and on
earth beneath.

---

6. the roof] See R.V. references to 1 S. ix. 25. A battle-
ment, or parapet, round the flat roof was ordered in Dt. xxii. 8
in the interests of safety.

the stalks of flax] Flax was a common plant in Palestine.
The stalks, some three feet in height, were placed on the roof to
dry, and resting slantwise against the parapet would afford a
fairly secure hiding-place.

10. the Amorites] Here the name is used of kingdoms E. of
the Jordan (cf. Numb. xxi. 13, 21), but generally in the O.T. it
refers to the inhabitants of the land W. of the river (vii. 7-9,
xxiv. 15, 18) and is identical with *Canaanite* (i.e. pre-Israelite
inhabitant of the land).

Og] A king of Bashan (see on xii. 5) whose name does not
enter Hebrew story till Deuteronomic times, and who was always
associated with Sihon (xii. 4, 5, Num. xxi. 33-35, Dt. iii. 1-11,
Ps. cxxxv. 11).

12–21. The agreement between Rahab and the spies.

Now therefore, I pray you, swear unto me by the LORD, 12
since I have dealt kindly with you, that ye also will
deal kindly with my father's house, and give me a true
token : and that ye will save alive my father, and my 13
mother, and my brethren, and my sisters, and all that they
have, and will deliver our lives from death. And the 14
men said unto her, Our life for yours, if ye utter not this
our business ; and it shall be, when the LORD giveth
us the land, that we will deal kindly and truly with thee.
Then she let them down by a cord through the window : 15
for her house was upon the town wall, and she dwelt
upon the wall. And she said unto them, Get you to 16

---

12. my father's house] i.e. my family and kindred (vi. 23).
It is the common expression for a sub-division of a tribe (xiv. 1),
but is used in xxii. 14 of the tribe itself.

a true token] In one of the versions of the story Rahab asks
for "a true token," that is, for some guarantee of good faith
(see on *v.* 18), while in the other she is content with the oath.
See on vi. 17.

14. The oath of the spies is to the effect that if Rahab maintains
secrecy her life will be safe ; they would sooner forfeit their
own.

for yours] marg. "Heb. *instead of you to die.*"

15. The spies who had been hidden on the roof are brought
into the house and let down from a window. It is, however,
more probable that the hiding *on the roof* and the escape by the
window are independent details of the two versions of the story
(see next verse).

a cord] This cord, or rope, is distinct from the *line* of
vv. 18, 21.

16. The long conversation (*vv.* 16–21) can hardly have taken
place under the conditions assumed in the text. The utmost
secrecy would have been necessary : and yet Rahab is apparently
at the window and the men on the ground. The difficulty is
removed by remembering that we are dealing with a combination
of two accounts, one of which records a conversation on the roof,
and the other a conversation in the house which must have preceded the escape by the window.

the mountain, lest the pursuers light upon you; and
hide yourselves there three days, until the pursuers be
17 returned: and afterward may ye go your way. And the
men said unto her, We will be guiltless of this thine oath
18 which thou hast made us to swear. Behold, when we
come into the land, thou shalt bind this line of scarlet
thread in the window which thou didst let us down by:
and thou shalt gather unto thee into the house thy father,
and thy mother, and thy brethren, and all thy father's
19 household. And it shall be, that whosoever shall go out
of the doors of thy house into the street, his blood shall
be upon his head, and we will be guiltless: and whosoever shall be with thee in the house, his blood shall be on
20 our head, if any hand be upon him. But if thou utter
this our business, then we will be guiltless of thine oath
21 which thou hast made us to swear. And she said,
According unto your words, so be it. And she sent them
away, and they departed: and she bound the scarlet line
in the window.

---

to the mountain] i.e. to the highlands of Judah which were
close by and contained secure retreats. Cf. xi. 16.

light upon]="come by chance upon." See on xv. 18.

17. We will be guiltless etc.] These words, as they stand,
must be an introduction to the three following verses:—"The
oath is not binding if you do not make use of the signal (*v.* 18 *a*),
see that your relatives are with you in your house (*vv.* 18 *b*, 19),
and keep the matter secret (*v.* 20). If these conditions are ful-
filled we guarantee your safety, but not otherwise." But it is
more probable that the words have been inserted here from
v. 20.

18. this line of scarlet thread] In Gen. xxxviii. 18 we read
of Judah's "signet" and "cord." The former was suspended
round the neck by the latter—a custom still in vogue amongst
well-to-do Arabs. It was this cord that the spy handed to
Rahab as "a true token," in the same way as Judah had done to
Tamar.

which thou didst let us down by] These words were added
by the writer who combined the two versions which mentioned,
respectively, the personal ornament of the spy, and the rope by
which the escape was effected.

22-24. The safe return of the spies and their report to Joshua.

And they went, and came unto the mountain, and abode 22
there three days, until the pursuers were returned : and
the pursuers sought them throughout all the way, but
found them not.   Then the two men returned, and de- 23
scended from the mountain, and passed over, and came
to Joshua the son of Nun ; and they told him all that
had befallen them.   And they said unto Joshua, Truly 24
the LORD hath delivered into our hands all the land ; and
moreover all the inhabitants of the land do melt away
before us.

iii. 1-13. *Removal from Shittim and arrival at the Jordan,*
   where Joshua, under the guidance of God, gives directions
   for crossing the river.

Chapters iii. and iv. contain a composite account of the
crossing of the Jordan.   There were evidently varying traditions
amongst the Israelites as to what actually took place on this
important occasion in their national history, but the story shows
how firmly the belief was rooted in their minds that God, who
had led his people through the dangers of the wilderness, did not
fail them on their entrance to the promised land.

And Joshua rose up early in the morning, and they 3
removed from Shittim, and came to Jordan, he and all
the children of Israel ; and they lodged there before they
passed over.   And it came to pass after three days, that 2
the officers went through the midst of the camp ; and 3
they commanded the people, saying, When ye see the ark

iii. 3.   The ark was designated by the earliest writers simply as
"the ark" (*v.* 15, Num. x. 35), or "the ark of the LORD"
(*v.* 13), or "the ark of God" (1 S. iii. 3).   In Deuteronomic
times we find "the ark of the covenant of the LORD" (as here,
Dt. xxxi. 9), and in still later times "the ark of the testimony"
(iv. 16), in both of which expressions there is a reference to the
two tables of stone which (Dt. x. 1-5) were placed in it.   What
the ark originally contained is not known, but it was always
regarded as the symbol of the presence of God (cf. on vi. 8).

of the covenant of the LORD your God, and the priests the
Levites bearing it, then ye shall remove from your place,
4 and go after it. Yet there shall be a space between you
and it, about two thousand cubits by measure : come not
near unto it, that ye may know the way by which ye must
5 go ; for ye have not passed this way heretofore. And
Joshua said unto the people, Sanctify yourselves : for to-
6 morrow the LORD will do wonders among you. And
Joshua spake unto the priests, saying, Take up the ark of
the covenant, and pass over before the people. And they
took up the ark of the covenant, and went before the
7 people. And the LORD said unto Joshua, This day will I
begin to magnify thee in the sight of all Israel, that they
may know that, as I was with Moses, so I will be with
8 thee. And thou shalt command the priests that bear the
ark of the covenant, saying, When ye are come to the
brink of the waters of Jordan, ye shall stand still in
Jordan.

9 And Joshua said unto the children of Israel, Come
10 hither, and hear the words of the LORD your God. And
Joshua said, Hereby ye shall know that the living God is

---

the priests the Levites] Every member of the tribe of Levi,
according to the older tradition, was a priest, and the carriage
of the ark was one of the special duties laid upon this tribe
(Dt. x. 8, xxxi. 9). In later times, when a distinction was made
between *priests* and *Levites*, the ark was entrusted to the latter
(Num. iii. 31, iv. 4, 5, 15, 1 Chron. xv. 2).

4. Yet there shall be...unto it] A later insertion, which
must be read as a parenthesis. A cubit is 1½ feet.

5. Sanctify yourselves] Cf. vii. 13, xxii. 19. On the present
occasion the people were bidden to prepare themselves, perhaps
by washing the body and a change of garments (Gen. xxxv. 2,
Ex. xix. 10–15), for the fighting, in which they were to be
associated with the sacred ark.

8. to the brink] So *v.* 15. Another tradition makes the
priests stand in the midst of the river (*vv.* 13, 17, iv. 3).

10. the living God] a living god. God lives and shows
that he lives by his works (see on i. 1). The people would have

among you, and that he will without fail drive out from
before you the Canaanite, and the Hittite, and the Hivite,
and the Perizzite, and the Girgashite, and the Amorite,
and the Jebusite.   Behold, the ark of the covenant of the 11
Lord of all the earth passeth over before you into Jordan.
Now therefore take you twelve men out of the tribes of 12
Israel, for every tribe a man.   And it shall come to pass, 13
when the soles of the feet of the priests that bear the ark
of the LORD, the Lord of all the earth, shall rest in the
waters of Jordan, that the waters of Jordan shall be cut
off, even the waters that come down from above ; and
they shall stand in one heap.

14-17.   *The people pass safely over while the waters of the
Jordan are held back.*

And it came to pass, when the people removed from 14
their tents, to pass over Jordan, the priests that bare the
ark of the covenant being before the people ; and when 15
they that bare the ark were come unto Jordan, and the
feet of the priests that bare the ark were dipped in

---

clear evidence (*v.* 13), as their fathers had (Ex. vi. 6, 7), of the
active existence of their God.

For **the Canaanite** and **Amorite** see on ii. 10, for **the Hittite** on
i. 4, and for **the Perizzite** on xvii. 15.   **The Hivite** appears as a
petty people living in the centre of the land (ix. 3, 7, xi. 19).
Nothing is known of **the Girgashite**, though mentioned in
Gen. x. 16 etc.   **The Jebusite** inhabited Jerusalem (x. 1).

12.   Repeated as a command of God in iv. 2.

13.   According to this verse the waters were to form a kind of
wall (cf. Ex. xiv. 22, xv. 8) just above the spot where the crossing
was to be made ; but in *v.* 16 the stoppage occurred some
distance off.

14-16 form a heavy sentence in which details from different
accounts are massed together.

15.   The normal course of the Jordan is through a deep bed.
But in the month of April-May, the time of harvest, it occasionally overflows the banks of this bed owing to the melting
of the snow at its sources, and floods the adjoining land.   The
mention of the overflow is intended to emphasize the miracle.

the brink of the water, (for Jordan overfloweth all its
16 banks all the time of harvest,) that the waters which
came down from above stood, and rose up in one heap,
a great way off, at Adam, the city that is beside Zarethan : and those that went down toward the sea of the
Arabah, even the Salt Sea, were wholly cut off : and the
17 people passed over right against Jericho.   And the
priests that bare the ark of the covenant of the LORD
stood firm on dry ground in the midst of Jordan, and all
Israel passed over on dry ground, until all the nation
were passed clean over Jordan.

> iv. 1–10 a. *Joshua sends twelve men back to bring up from the
> middle of the Jordan twelve stones to serve as a memorial
> at Gilgal.   He also sets up twelve stones in the bed of the
> Jordan to mark the resting-place of the ark.*

4   And it came to pass, when all the nation were clean
passed over Jordan, that the LORD spake unto Joshua,
2 saying, Take you twelve men out of the people, out of
3 every tribe a man, and command ye them, saying, Take
you hence out of the midst of Jordan, out of the place
where the priests' feet stood firm, twelve stones, and carry

---

16.   Adam] probably *tell ed-Dāmije*, which lies on the left
bank of the Jordan about 15 miles north of the ford by Jericho :
and **Zarethan** is thought to be *Ḳarn Ṣarṭabe*, on the bank just
opposite to it.

The Arabah is "the deep valley running North and South of
the Dead Sea."   **The sea of the Arabah** is the Dead Sea, though
it is never called by the latter name in the Bible.   The name **Salt
Sea** is given to it from the large quantity of salt which is held in
solution and which accounts for the absence of life in its waters ;
a few small fish only have been seen.

17.   clean] i.e. completely.   So Ps. lxxvii. 8, Is xxiv. 19.

iv. 3.   Take you]   In this account twelve representative men
take up the stones ; in *v.* 8, "the children of Israel" take them.

stones]   These could only have been small (*v.* 5), and twelve
would have been of little use for memorial purposes.   If the
account in *v.* 8 be the correct one, twelve large stones could have
been taken up and a suitable memorial erected.

Memorial stones are frequently mentioned in the O.T., them over with you, and lay them down in the lodging place, where ye shall lodge this night. Then Joshua 4 called the twelve men, whom he had prepared of the children of Israel, out of every tribe a man : and Joshua 5 said unto them, Pass over before the ark of the LORD your God into the midst of Jordan, and take you up every man of you a stone upon his shoulder, according unto the number of the tribes of the children of Israel : that this 6 may be a sign among you, that when your children ask in time to come, saying, What mean ye by these stones? then ye shall say unto them, Because the waters of Jordan 7 were cut off before the ark of the covenant of the LORD ; when it passed over Jordan, the waters of Jordan were cut off : and these stones shall be for a memorial unto the children of Israel for ever. And the children of 8 Israel did so as Joshua commanded, and took up twelve stones out of the midst of Jordan, as the LORD spake unto Joshua, according to the number of the tribes of the children of Israel ; and they carried them over with them unto the place where they lodged, and laid them down there. And Joshua set up twelve stones in the midst of 9

---

either singly (xxiv. 26, Gen. xxviii. 18), or as "heaps" (vii. 26, viii. 29, Gen. xxxi. 46), or as "circles" (*v.* 19). Many of them dated back long before the Israelite conquest and were held to be so sacred that there was no thought of destroying them ; on the contrary, in course of time they came to be regarded as symbols of the presence of Jehovah. The stories of Jacob's pillar at Bethel and Joshua's stones at Gilgal and Shechem are attempts to associate pre-Israelite relics with the worship of Jehovah. Cf. also on xv. 6.

5. before] i.e. in the presence of (as in *v.* 11), implying "under the protection of."

6, 7. Another explanation, by a different writer, is given in *vv.* 21-24.

6. when your children ask etc.] Cf. Ex. xii. 26, xiii. 14, Dt. vi. 20.

9. It is possible that some stones set up to mark the ford of the Jordan at this spot may have given rise to the belief that Joshua placed them there to commemorate his crossing.

Jordan, in the place where the feet of the priests which bare the ark of the covenant stood : and they are there,
10 unto this day. For the priests which bare the ark stood in the midst of Jordan, until every thing was finished that the LORD commanded Joshua to speak unto the people, according to all that Moses commanded Joshua :

10 *b*–19. *Concluding details of the crossing.*

11 and the people hasted and passed over. And it came to pass, when all the people were clean passed over, that the ark of the LORD passed over, and the priests, in the pres-
12 ence of the people. And the children of Reuben, and the children of Gad, and the half tribe of Manasseh, passed over armed before the children of Israel, as Moses spake
13 unto them : about forty thousand ready armed for war passed over before the LORD unto battle, to the plains of
14 Jericho. On that day the LORD magnified Joshua in the sight of all Israel ; and they feared him, as they feared Moses, all the days of his life.

15
16 And the LORD spake unto Joshua, saying, Command the priests that bear the ark of the testimony, that they
17 come up out of Jordan. Joshua therefore commanded
18 the priests, saying, Come ye up out of Jordan. And it came to pass, when the priests that bare the ark of the covenant of the LORD were come up out of the midst of

---

unto this day] Cf. v. 9, vi. 25, ix. 27 etc. The expression implies that there was some interval between the events and the record of them.

10. according to all etc.] No such commands have been preserved (cf. xv. 13, xix. 50).

10 *b*. Another account (iii. 17) has already stated that the crossing had been completed.

11. The ark is said to pass over here, and again in *vv.* 15–17 (two accounts).

13. about forty thousand] We have no means of ascertaining how the numbers in such passages as this were reached. The number of males belonging to the trans-Jordanic tribes, given in Num. xxvi., is much larger.

Jordan, and the soles of the priests' feet were lifted up
unto the dry ground, that the waters of Jordan returned
unto their place, and went over all its banks, as aforetime.
And the people came up out of Jordan on the tenth day 19
of the first month, and encamped in Gilgal, on the east
border of Jericho.

20–24. *A second explanation of the memorial stones at Gilgal.*

And those twelve stones, which they took out of Jordan, 20
did Joshua set up in Gilgal. And he spake unto the 21
children of Israel, saying, When your children shall ask
their fathers in time to come, saying, What mean these
stones? then ye shall let your children know, saying, 22
Israel came over this Jordan on dry land. For the 23
LORD your God dried up the waters of Jordan from
before you, until ye were passed over, as the LORD
your God did to the Red Sea, which he dried up from
before us, until we were passed over : that all the peoples 24

---

19. A precise statement by a late writer (cf. v. 10, Gen. viii. 13),
who in accordance with his custom simply designates the month
numerically. The first month (April-May) was originally called
Abib, the month of the ripe "ear." In later times it received
the Babylonian name Nisan.

Gilgal] The name, which means "a circle" (of stones), is
used of other places besides that intended here; but this is the
most important. It lay about 2 miles S.E. of Jericho, and was
an old Canaanite sanctuary, which was held in much repute in
later times (Hos. iv. 15). Joshua used the place as a military
base (see on viii. 3).

20. those] Heb. **these**, showing that this verse was not
originally separated from the account of the erection of the stones
in *vv.* 1–8.

23, 24 are probably a continuation of the instruction to be
given to the children. Cf. the similar passages Ex. xiii. 14–16,
Dt. vi. 20–25.

23. dried up] As, according to one account, the spot where
the waters were cut off was some distance from the place where
the Israelites crossed (iii. 16), it would seem to them as if the
waters had been dried up.

of the earth may know the hand of the LORD, that it is
mighty ; that they may fear the LORD your God for ever.

*v. 1. Effect of the crossing of the Jordan on the spirit of the
native kings.*

5   And it came to pass, when all the kings of the Amorites,
which were beyond Jordan westward, and all the kings of
the Canaanites, which were by the sea, heard how that
the LORD had dried up the waters of Jordan from before
the children of Israel, until we were passed over, that
their heart melted, neither was there spirit in them any
more, because of the children of Israel.

*2–12. Religious ceremonies at Gilgal : Circumcision and the
Passover.*

2   At that time the LORD said unto Joshua, Make thee
knives of flint, and circumcise again the children of Israel
3 the second time. And Joshua made him knives of flint,
and circumcised the children of Israel at the hill of the
4 foreskins. And this is the cause why Joshua did circumcise : all the people that came forth out of Egypt, that
were males, even all the men of war, died in the wilderness
5 by the way, after they came forth out of Egypt. For all
the people that came out were circumcised : but all the
people that were born in the wilderness by the way as
they came forth out of Egypt, they had not circumcised.
6 For the children of Israel walked forty years in the

---

v. 2. knives of flint] Cf. Ex. iv. 25. Implements of flint
were used by the Israelites long after they had entered Canaan.
On the introduction of iron see at vi. 19.

circumcise again...the second time] This does not agree with
v. 7; **again...the second time** has probably been inserted by an
editor who could not understand how circumcision, said to have
been instituted in patriarchal times (Gen. xvii.), could ever have
been neglected.

3. the hill of the foreskins] Perhaps a proper name *Gibeath-
ha-araloth.* Cf. xxiv. 33.

wilderness, till all the nation, even the men of war which came forth out of Egypt, were consumed, because they hearkened not unto the voice of the LORD : unto whom the LORD sware that he would not let them see the land which the LORD sware unto their fathers that he would give us, a land flowing with milk and honey. And their 7 children, whom he raised up in their stead, them did Joshua circumcise : for they were uncircumcised, because they had not circumcised them by the way. And it came 8 to pass, when they had done circumcising all the nation, that they abode in their places in the camp, till they were whole. And the LORD said unto Joshua, This day 9 have I rolled away the reproach of Egypt from off you. Wherefore the name of that place was called Gilgal, unto this day.

And the children of Israel encamped in Gilgal ; and 10 they kept the passover on the fourteenth day of the month at even in the plains of Jericho. And they did eat of the 11 old corn of the land on the morrow after the passover, unleavened cakes and parched corn, in the selfsame day. And the manna ceased on the morrow, after they had 12

---

6. **a land flowing** etc.] i.e. a very fertile land. The honey of wild bees was plentiful in Palestine (1 S. xiv. 27, Matt. iii. 4), but it is possible that the reference is to a sweet syrup made from grapes, such as is in common use to-day.

9. As *gallōthi* (= "I have rolled away") and *Gilgal* are derived from the same root the writer states that the place received its name from the "rolling away" of the reproach. But Gilgal existed long before Joshua's day and the name means "a circle" (of stones). See at iv. 19.

the reproach of Egypt] is that thrown by the Egyptians, who were circumcised, at the uncircumcised Israelites.

10–12. By the same writer as iv. 19.

The Passover was kept by the Israelites from primitive times ; the earliest rules for its observance are found in Ex. xii. 21–23.

11. **old corn**] **produce** (so *v.* 12), i.e. the grain of that year's harvest (iii. 15).

12. **manna**] There is a substance produced by the tamarisk

eaten of the old corn of the land ; neither had the children
of Israel manna any more ; but they did eat of the fruit
of the land of Canaan that year.

13–15. *Joshua and the captain of the host of the LORD.*

13   And it came to pass, when Joshua was by Jericho, that
he lifted up his eyes and looked, and, behold, there
stood a man over against him with his sword drawn in
his hand : and Joshua went unto him, and said unto him,
14 Art thou for us, or for our adversaries ? And he said,
Nay ; but *as* captain of the host of the LORD am I now
come. And Joshua fell on his face to the earth, and did
worship, and said unto him, What saith my lord unto his
15 servant ? And the captain of the LORD's host said unto
Joshua, Put off thy shoe from off thy foot ; for the place
whereon thou standest is holy. And Joshua did so.

---

tree and called by the Arabs *mann* ; it is sweet to the taste and
liable soon to pall, and only found in small quantities. In all
the passages, however, where the manna is mentioned (with
the exception of Num. xi. 6–9) it is believed to be a miraculous
gift of God (e.g. Ex. xvi. 15, 35, Wisd. xvi. 20, John vi.
31, 32).

on the morrow] i.e. after the passover. The same day is
meant as in *v.* 11.

14. the host of the LORD] i.e. Jehovah's heavenly host
(1 K. xxii. 19, Is. xxiv. 21, Dan. viii. 10, 11), either the stars
(Jud. v. 20) or the angels (Gen. xxxii. 1, 2). **The host** (sc. of
heaven) must not be confounded with *hosts*, which frequently
occurs in the expression "the LORD of hosts" (i.e. the armies of
Israel). Cf. 1 S. xvii. 45.

worship] is apparently a noun (cf. Luke xiv. 10 A.V.), as the
past tense of the verb is elsewhere "worshipped."

15. Put off etc.] Moses received the same command when
God called him (Ex. iii. 5). Cf. 2 S. xv. 30.

vi. 1–5. *Joshua is instructed to make a processional march round Jericho.*

The story is composite. It seems probable that one tradition was to the effect that the men of war marched in silence round the city once a day for seven days and then took it by assault; while another, assigning high prominence to the ark and the priests, described a religious procession of the whole people, seven times in one day, accompanied by much blowing of horns. At the close the walls fell. The collapse of the walls is considered to be miraculous.

Nothing is said here of any counter-movement on the part of the inhabitants of Jericho, but according to xxiv. 11 they made some resistance.

(Now Jericho was straitly shut up because of the children **6** of Israel: none went out, and none came in.) And the **2** LORD said unto Joshua, See, I have given into thine hand Jericho, and the king thereof, and the mighty men of valour. And ye shall compass the city, all the men of **3** war, going about the city once. Thus shalt thou do six days. And seven priests shall bear seven trumpets of **4** rams' horns before the ark: and the seventh day ye shall compass the city seven times, and the priests shall blow with the trumpets. And it shall be, that when they make **5** a long blast with the ram's horn, and when ye hear the sound of the trumpet, all the people shall shout with a great shout; and the wall of the city shall fall down flat, and the people shall go up every man straight before him.

---

vi. 1. straitly] i.e. closely, from Lat. *strictus* = "drawn together." Cf. Gen. xliii. 7, Matt. vii. 13, 14.

4. In this verse (cf. *v.* 8) the priests are to blow the trumpets during the march. Contrast *v.* 10, where strict silence is enjoined.

seven] A number to which special sanctity was attached (Gen. vii. 2, Num. xxiii. 1).

trumpets of rams' horns] These were curved, and distinct from the straight metal trumpet (Num. x. 2).

5. Here the signal for the attack is a blast with the ram's horn; in *v.* 10 it is the command of Joshua. In *vv.* 16, 20 the two signals appear to be combined.

flat] in its place, as in v. 8, Jud. vii. 21.

6–14. The march on the first six days described.

6 And Joshua the son of Nun called the priests, and said
unto them, Take up the ark of the covenant, and let seven
priests bear seven trumpets of rams' horns before the ark
7 of the LORD. And they said unto the people, Pass on,
and compass the city, and let the armed men pass on
8 before the ark of the LORD. And it was so, that when
Joshua had spoken unto the people, the seven priests
bearing the seven trumpets of rams' horns before the LORD
passed on, and blew with the trumpets : and the ark of
9 the covenant of the LORD followed them. And the armed
men went before the priests that blew the trumpets, and
the rearward went after the ark, *the priests* blowing with
10 the trumpets as they went. And Joshua commanded the
people, saying, Ye shall not shout, nor let your voice be
heard, neither shall any word proceed out of your mouth,
11 until the day I bid you shout ; then shall ye shout. So
he caused the ark of the LORD to compass the city, going
about it once : and they came into the camp, and lodged
in the camp.

12 And Joshua rose early in the morning, and the priests
13 took up the ark of the LORD. And the seven priests
bearing the seven trumpets of rams' horns before the ark
of the LORD went on continually, and blew with the
trumpets : and the armed men went before them ; and
the rearward came after the ark of the LORD, *the priests*
14 blowing with the trumpets as they went. And the second
day they compassed the city once, and returned into the
camp : so they did six days.

---

7. **they said**] A better reading is *he said*.
8. **before the LORD**] These words show how closely God's
presence was associated with the ark (see on iii. 3).

*15–21.   The march on the seventh day and the devoting of
the city.*

And it came to pass on the seventh day, that they rose 15
early at the dawning of the day, and compassed the city
after the same manner seven times : only on that day
they compassed the city seven times.   And it came to 16
pass at the seventh time, when the priests blew with the
trumpets, Joshua said unto the people, Shout ; for the
LORD hath given you the city.   And the city shall be 17
devoted, even it and all that is therein, to the LORD :
only Rahab the harlot shall live, she and all that are
with her in the house, because she hid the messengers
that we sent.   And ye, in any wise keep yourselves from 18
the devoted thing, lest when ye have devoted it, ye take
of the devoted thing ; so should ye make the camp of
Israel accursed, and trouble it.   But all the silver, and 19
gold, and vessels of brass and iron, are holy unto the
LORD : they shall come into the treasury of the LORD.

---

17.   devoted] i.e. surrendered to the exclusive use of God
(cf. vii. 23).   The word is chiefly used of the extermination of
life ; hence the alternative rendering *utterly destroy* (e.g. *v.* 21).

It is implied in the present verse (cf. *v.* 25) that Rahab and her
family remained in the house during the assault. . This would agree
with that version of the story (ii. 12, 18) which mentions the
token that would lead to the recognition of the house and the
sparing of its inmates amidst the general slaughter.   On the
other hand *vv.* 22, 23 state that the two spies, who of course
would know the house and would not require any scarlet line to
guide them, had been sent to the house some time previously in
order to convey Rahab to a place of safety, in accordance with
their oath (cf. ii. 14, 20).

18.   wise] i.e. way, manner (Ex. xxii. 23, Matt. i. 18).

19.   brass] **copper** (or **bronze**, an alloy of copper and tin).
Brass, an alloy of copper and zinc, was not known till later times.

iron]   The use of iron is not attested by the excavations in
Palestine till *c.* B.C. 1000.   The mention of it here (and *v.* 24,
xvii. 16, xxii. 8) is probably an anachronism.

the treasury of the LORD]=**the treasury of the house** etc.
(*v.* 24).   Not the Temple at Jerusalem, but a sanctuary, perhaps
at Gilgal.

20 So the people shouted, and *the priests* blew with the trumpets : and it came to pass, when the people heard the sound of the trumpet, that the people shouted with a great shout, and the wall fell down flat, so that the people went up into the city, every man straight before him, and
21 they took the city. And they utterly destroyed all that was in the city, both man and woman, both young and old, and ox, and sheep, and ass, with the edge of the sword.

22–27. Rahab and her family are spared, and Joshua pronounces a curse upon the man who builds Jericho again.

22 And Joshua said unto the two men that had spied out the land, Go into the harlot's house, and bring out thence the woman, and all that she hath, as ye sware unto
23 her. And the young men the spies went in, and brought out Rahab, and her father, and her mother, and her brethren, and all that she had, all her kindred also they brought out ; and they set them without the camp of
24 Israel. And they burnt the city with fire, and all that was therein : only the silver, and the gold, and the vessels of brass and of iron, they put into the treasury of the
25 house of the LORD. But Rahab the harlot, and her father's household, and all that she had, did Joshua save alive ; and she dwelt in the midst of Israel, unto this day ; because she hid the messengers, which Joshua sent to spy
26 out Jericho. And Joshua charged them with an oath at that time, saying, Cursed be the man before the LORD, that riseth up and buildeth this city Jericho : with the

---

22. And Joshua said] **Now Joshua had said.** The command must have been given and performed while the house was standing.
26. buildeth] Jericho, though devoted by Joshua, was soon re-inhabited (see on ii. 1). The curse must therefore be taken to refer to the man who should fortify it. See 1 K. xvi. 34 for its supposed fulfilment (Driver, *Modern Research*, p. 72).

loss of his firstborn shall he lay the foundation thereof, and with the loss of his youngest son shall he set up the gates of it.   So the LORD was with Joshua ; and his fame was 27 in all the land.

vii. 1.   *The sin of Achan.*

But the children of Israel committed a trespass in the **7** devoted thing : for Achan, the son of Carmi, the son of Zabdi, the son of Zerah, of the tribe of Judah, took of the devoted thing : and the anger of the LORD was kindled against the children of Israel.

2–5.   *Three thousand Israelites are repulsed at Ai.*

And Joshua sent men from Jericho to Ai, which is 2 beside Beth-aven, on the east side of Beth-el, and spake unto them, saying, Go up and spy out the land.   And the men went up and spied out Ai.   And they returned to 3 Joshua, and said unto him, Let not all the people go up ; but let about two or three thousand men go up and smite

---

27.   his fame] i.e. the fame of the LORD (ix. 9 ; cf. ii. 10).

vii. 1.   the anger of the LORD was kindled]   as the narrative itself shows ; for no word nor command of God is mentioned till after the disaster at Ai has taken place.   God is angry, and silent.

2.   sent...from Jericho] i.e. immediately after its "devotion." The camp was still at Gilgal (see on viii. 3).   **Beth-el** lies about ten miles N. of Jerusalem, and **Ai** about two miles S.E. of Beth-el, on the road from Jericho.   It is possible that **which is beside Beth-aven** is merely a gloss on the words **on the east side of Beth-el**.

Probably the historical kernel of the present story is that the first Israelite attack on Ai failed because it was made on imperfect information and in a spirit of overweening confidence, engendered by the success at Jericho.   The story of Achan and the infringement of the "devotion" has been used to mask the strategical error on the part of Joshua of sending 3000 men to attack a walled city defended by a larger number (four to five thousand, viii. 25).

Ai; make not all the people to toil thither; for they are
4 but few. So there went up thither of the people about
three thousand men: and they fled before the men of Ai.
5 And the men of Ai smote of them about thirty and six
men: and they chased them *from* before the gate even
unto Shebarim, and smote them at the going down: and
the hearts of the people melted, and became as water.

6–9. *Joshua's lament.*

6 And Joshua rent his clothes, and fell to the earth upon
his face before the ark of the LORD until the evening,
he and the elders of Israel; and they put dust upon
7 their heads. And Joshua said, Alas, O Lord GOD, wherefore hast thou at all brought this people over Jordan,
to deliver us into the hand of the Amorites, to cause us
to perish? would that we had been content and dwelt
8 beyond Jordan! Oh Lord, what shall I say, after that
9 Israel hath turned their backs before their enemies! For
the Canaanites and all the inhabitants of the land shall
hear of it, and shall compass us round, and cut off our
name from the earth: and what wilt thou do for thy
great name?

10–15. *God declares that the cause of the repulse is the sin of Achan and instructs Joshua how to discover and punish the culprit.*

10 And the LORD said unto Joshua, Get thee up; wherefore
11 art thou thus fallen upon thy face? Israel hath sinned;

4, 5. These verses read as if they were based on two separate
accounts; for in *v.* 4 the Israelites fled before the men of Ai, and
in *v.* 5 they are still being chased *before the gate* of the city.

5. Shebarim] No place of this name is known. As marg.
("Or, *the quarries*") implies, the word may not be a proper noun.
the going down] i.e. the descent from the city.

6. the elders] heads of large families or clans, corresponding
to the present Sheiks.

9. and what wilt thou do etc.?] If Israel is cut off Jehovah
will have no worshippers and his character will be tarnished.

yea, they have even transgressed my covenant which I commanded them : yea, they have even taken of the devoted thing ; and have also stolen, and dissembled also, and they have even put it among their own stuff. Therefore 12 the children of Israel cannot stand before their enemies, they turn their backs before their enemies, because they are become accursed : I will not be with you any more, except ye destroy the devoted thing from among you. Up, sanctify the people, and say, Sanctify yourselves 13 against to-morrow : for thus saith the LORD, the God of Israel, There is a devoted thing in the midst of thee, O Israel : thou canst not stand before thine enemies, until ye take away the devoted thing from among you. In the 14 morning therefore ye shall be brought near by your tribes : and it shall be, that the tribe which the LORD taketh shall come near by families ; and the family which the LORD shall take shall come near by households ; and the household which the LORD shall take shall come near man by man. And it shall be, that he that is taken with 15 the devoted thing shall be burnt with fire, he and all that he hath : because he hath transgressed the covenant of the LORD, and because he hath wrought folly in Israel.

---

11. covenant] The Heb. word virtually means "command," "injunction" (as here, and *v.* 15, xxiv. 25), as well as "agreement" (Dt. xxix. 12).

stuff] Properly, "what may be stuffed (stowed) away." In Biblical use it means "baggage," "moveable goods." See Gen. xxxi. 37, 1 S. xxv. 13.

14. ye shall be brought near by your tribes] The head man of each tribe, as its representative, was to appear before the Lord (cf. 1 S. x. 19–21), i.e. probably before the ark, so that the ceremony of investigation and detection might be carried out both in public and with due solemnity.

15. wrought] past tense of "to work," and originally the only form ; but "worked" is used now. For the expression **wrought folly** cf. Gen. xxxiv. 7, Jud. xix. 23, 24.

16-26. Discovery of the culprit and his punishment.

16 So Joshua rose up early in the morning, and brought
Israel near by their tribes ; and the tribe of Judah was
17 taken : and he brought near the family of Judah ; and he
took the family of the Zerahites : and he brought near the
family of the Zerahites man by man ; and Zabdi was
18 taken : and he brought near his household man by man ;
and Achan, the son of Carmi, the son of Zabdi, the son
19 of Zerah, of the tribe of Judah, was taken. And Joshua
said unto Achan, My son, give, I pray thee, glory to the
LORD, the God of Israel, and make confession unto him ;
and tell me now what thou hast done ; hide it not from
20 me. And Achan answered Joshua, and said, Of a truth
I have sinned against the LORD, the God of Israel, and
21 thus and thus have I done : when I saw among the spoil
a goodly Babylonish mantle, and two hundred shekels of
silver, and a wedge of gold of fifty shekels weight, then I
coveted them, and took them ; and, behold, they are hid in
the earth in the midst of my tent, and the silver under it.
22 So Joshua sent messengers, and they ran unto the tent ;
and, behold, it was hid in his tent, and the silver under
23 it. And they took them from the midst of the tent, and
brought them unto Joshua, and unto all the children of

---

19. Though he stands convicted of the theft Achan is exhorted
to acknowledge that the result of the investigation is a proof of
Jehovah's power and justice (cf. 1 S. vi. 5). But the verse also
seems to express the thankfulness of Joshua, that as the cause of
the recent repulse is discovered Jehovah will soon again " be
with " his people (*v.* 12).

make confession] Rather, as marg., **give praise** : so Ezra
x. 11. Cf. John ix. 24.

20. thus and thus] an abbreviation by an editor (cf. 2 S.
xvii. 15, 2 K. v. 4). The details of the theft were probably given
here but omitted in favour of those now appearing, from another
version, in *v.* 21.

21. shekels] The shekel weighed about an ounce.

23. they laid them down] So LXX. The Heb. = " poured
them out."

Israel ; and they laid them down before the LORD.   And 24
Joshua, and all Israel with him, took Achan the son of
Zerah, and the silver, and the mantle, and the wedge
of gold, and his sons, and his daughters, and his oxen,
and his asses, and his sheep, and his tent, and all that
he had : and they brought them up unto the valley of
Achor.   And Joshua said, Why hast thou troubled us? 25
the LORD shall trouble thee this day.   And all Israel
stoned him with stones ; and they burned them with fire,
and stoned them with stones.   And they raised over him a 26
great heap of stones, unto this day ; and the LORD turned
from the fierceness of his anger.   Wherefore the name of
that place was called, The valley of Achor, unto this day.

viii. 1, 2.   *Joshua is instructed to take Ai by setting an
ambush.*

And the LORD said unto Joshua, Fear not, neither be 8
thou dismayed : take all the people of war with thee, and
arise, go up to Ai : see, I have given into thy hand the
king of Ai, and his people, and his city, and his land :
and thou shalt do to Ai and her king as thou didst unto 2
Jericho and her king : only the spoil thereof, and the
cattle thereof, shall ye take for a prey unto yourselves :
set thee an ambush for the city behind it.

---

before the LORD] Jehovah at last received what had been
devoted to him (vi. 17), but what Achan had impiously appro-
priated.

24.   the son] So xxii. 20.   In Heb. it is often used for a
descendant.

the valley of Achor] xv. 7, Is. lxv. 10, Hos. ii. 15.

25.   troubled...trouble] Cf. vi. 18.   There is a play on the
Heb. for *trouble* ('*akar*) and the name '*Achan*.

him ...them] There seem to have been two traditions as to
the method by which Achan was put to death, viz. stoning and
burning.   The two are here combined, and his family and possessions (*v* 24) are included in the punishment

viii. 2   **behind it**] i.e. to the west of it (*v.* 9).   So *vv.* 4, 14.

3-9. *The ambush is set and Joshua, with the main body, plans to feign defeat.*

3 So Joshua arose, and all the people of war, to go up to Ai: and Joshua chose out thirty thousand men, the mighty men
4 of valour, and sent them forth by night. And he commanded them, saying, Behold, ye shall lie in ambush against the city, behind the city: go not very far from the city, but
5 be ye all ready: and I, and all the people that are with me, will approach unto the city: and it shall come to pass, when they come out against us, as at the first, that
6 we will flee before them; and they will come out after us, till we have drawn them away from the city; for they will say, They flee before us, as at the first; so we will flee
7 before them: and ye shall rise up from the ambush, and take possession of the city: for the LORD your God will
8 deliver it into your hand. And it shall be, when ye have seized upon the city, that ye shall set the city on fire; according to the word of the LORD shall ye do: see, I
9 have commanded you. And Joshua sent them forth: and they went to the ambushment, and abode between Beth-el and Ai, on the west side of Ai: but Joshua lodged that night among the people.

---

3. So Joshua arose] i.e. from Gilgal, where the Israelite camp had been placed at the first (iv. 19) and which was used as a base for expeditions subsequent to that against Jericho (ix. 6, x. 15, 43). The first half of this verse mentions the start of Joshua from Gilgal to Ai; the second half, and *vv.* 4-9, state what he did when he reached Ai.

thirty thousand men] Such an army would equal in numbers that of Israel in David's time (2 S. vi. 1). There is evidently some mistake, and probably *three thousand* should be read. Cf. the 5000 of *v.* 12.

5. as at the first] The unsuccessful attack (vii. 4, 5) would have been made from the south as the Israelites would not have placed the city between themselves and their line of retreat. Joshua intends on the present occasion to approach the city from the same side.

9. lodged...among the people] These words should probably

10-13. *Another account of the setting of the ambush.*

In this second account Joshua musters the people at Gilgal and the march is made to Ai. The ambush is set on the W. of the city, but (contrast *v.* 3) it consists of five thousand men, while Joshua and the main body pitch on the N. side (contrast *v.* 5).

And Joshua rose up early in the morning, and mustered 10 the people, and went up, he and the elders of Israel, before the people to Ai. And all the people, *even* the 11 *men of* war that were with him, went up, and drew nigh, and came before the city, and pitched on the north side of Ai : now there was a valley between him and Ai. And 12 he took about five thousand men, and set them in ambush between Beth-el and Ai, on the west side of the city. So 13 they set the people, even all the host that was on the north of the city, and their liers in wait that were on the west of the city ; and Joshua went that night into the midst of the vale.

14-29. *The people of Ai, after leaving the city in pursuit of the Israelites, find themselves between the ambush, which had taken the city, and the main body, and are cut off to a man. The city is devoted.*

And it came to pass, when the king of Ai saw it, that 14 they hasted and rose up early, and the men of the city went out against Israel to battle, he and all his people, at the time appointed, before the Arabah ; but he wist not that there was an ambush against him behind the city. And Joshua and all Israel made as if they were beaten 15 before them, and fled by the way of the wilderness.

---

be *went...into the midst of the vale*, as in *v.* 13 which closes the second account of the setting of the ambush etc. The two expressions in the Heb. differ only by two letters.

13. their liers in wait] their rear.

14. at the time appointed] Neither *time* nor *place* (marg.) seems suitable. Perhaps the original was *at the going down* (as in vii. 5), a very similar word in the Heb.

before] i.e. towards.

15. made as if they were beaten] were beaten. There are two versions of the fight at Ai. In one version (of which this verse

16 And all the people that were in the city were called
together to pursue after them : and they pursued after
17 Joshua, and were drawn away from the city.   And there
was not a man left in Ai or Beth-el, that went not out
after Israel : and they left the city open, and pursued
18 after Israel.   And the LORD said unto Joshua, Stretch
out the javelin that is in thy hand toward Ai ; for I will
give it into thine hand.   And Joshua stretched out the
19 javelin that was in his hand toward the city.   And the
ambush arose quickly out of their place, and they ran
as soon as he had stretched out his hand, and entered
into the city, and took it ; and they hasted and set the city
20 on fire.   And when the men of Ai looked behind them,
they saw, and, behold, the smoke of the city ascended up
to heaven, and they had no power to flee this way or that
way : and the people that fled to the wilderness turned
21 back upon the pursuers.   And when Joshua and all
Israel saw that the ambush had taken the city, and that
the smoke of the city ascended, then they turned again,
22 and slew the men of Ai.   And the other came forth out
of the city against them ; so they were in the midst of

---

forms a part) the Israelites were worsted and had to flee.   The
flight was stayed by Joshua who at God's command stretched out
the javelin that was in his hand ; and the success of Israel was
assured by his arm remaining outstretched (*v.* 26).   Cf. the
story of Moses, Ex. xvii. 11.

In the other version the Israelites made a pretence of being
worsted, thus drawing the men of Ai out of their city.   When
the ambush took the city the column of rising smoke became
the signal to Joshua that it was time to "turn again," for the
stratagem had been completely successful.

It was the task of the editor to combine these two versions,
and in doing so he has made it appear (*v.* 19 "as soon as he had
stretched out his hand ") that the javelin of Joshua was the signal
for the ambush.

by the way of the wilderness] i.e. towards the rugged country
which commences about two miles from Ai and continues eastward as far as the Arabah.

Israel, some on this side, and some on that side : and they smote them, so that they let none of them remain or escape. And the king of Ai they took alive, and brought 23 him to Joshua And it came to pass, when Israel had 24 made an end of slaying all the inhabitants of Ai in the field, in the wilderness wherein they pursued them, and they were all fallen by the edge of the sword, until they were consumed, that all Israel returned unto Ai, and smote it with the edge of the sword. And all that fell 25 that day, both of men and women, were twelve thousand, even all the men of Ai. For Joshua drew not back his 26 hand, wherewith he stretched out the javelin, until he had utterly destroyed all the inhabitants of Ai. Only the 27 cattle and the spoil of that city Israel took for a prey unto themselves, according unto the word of the LORD which he commanded Joshua. So Joshua burnt Ai, and made 28 it an heap for ever, even a desolation, unto this day. And the king of Ai he hanged on a tree until the eventide : 29 and at the going down of the sun Joshua commanded, and they took his carcase down from the tree, and cast it at the entering of the gate of the city, and raised thereon a great heap of stones, unto this day.

30–35. *Joshua builds an altar on Mt. Ebal and writes the law of Moses on stones. Afterwards he reads the law to the Israelites assembled on Mts. Ebal and Gerizim.*

The two mountains mentioned here are in the centre of the land and about twenty miles N. of Ai. The valley between them, in which was the important town of Shechem (xx. 7), lies S.E. and N.W., and in the neighbourhood of Shechem

---

24. in the field] i.e. the more level and open country close to Ai.

28. heap] marg. "Or, *mound* Heb. *tel*": see on xi. 13. Ai was, like Jericho, afterwards rebuilt (Is. x. 28).

29. hanged] From x. 26 we gather that it was the dead body of the king that was thus exposed to public contempt.

a great heap [Heb. *gal*] **of stones**] See on iv. 3.

is not more than 500 yards wide. The performance of the ceremonies implies that the mountains and the surrounding district were in the hands of the Israelites. Nothing, however, has hitherto been mentioned of the conquest of Central Palestine.

It has therefore been suggested that this section should be placed later in the book (after xi. 23), or that the editor has omitted the record of the conquest that would make possible the events here described.

But even though a suitable context be found for it, it can hardly claim to be an historical record, in its present form, of what took place in the days of Joshua. The building of the altar may be the historical element of the story (cf. Ex. xx. 24, 25), but this has been amplified by writers of the Deuteronomic School. With *vv*. 30–32 compare Dt. xxvii. 1–8, and with *vv*. 33–35, Dt. xi. 29, xxvii. 12, 13, xxxi. 9–13.

30   Then Joshua built an altar unto the LORD, the God of
31 Israel, in Mount Ebal, as Moses the servant of the LORD commanded the children of Israel, as it is written in the book of the law of Moses, an altar of unhewn stones, upon which no man had lift up any iron : and they offered thereon burnt offerings unto the LORD, and sacrificed
32 peace offerings. And he wrote there upon the stones a copy of the law of Moses, which he wrote, in the presence
33 of the children of Israel. And all Israel, and their elders and officers, and their judges, stood on this side the ark and on that side before the priests the Levites, which bare the ark of the covenant of the LORD, as well the stranger as the homeborn ; half of them in front of mount Gerizim, and half of them in front of mount Ebal ; as Moses the servant of the LORD had commanded, that they should

---

31. book of the law] Cf. *vv*. 32, 34. See on i. 8.

32. the stones] i.e. of the altar. But we are probably meant to understand them by a reference to Dt. xxvii. 2. The stones would be plastered (with lime) and the words written on the plaster.

33. the stranger] one of alien birth settled in Israel. He is frequently mentioned in Israelite legislation and careful provision is made for his rights (e.g. Dt. v. 14).

Gerizim] celebrated in post-exilic times as the spot on which the Samaritans built their temple (cf. John iv. 20).

bless the people of Israel first of all. And afterward he 34
read all the words of the law, the blessing and the curse,
according to all that is written in the book of the law.
There was not a word of all that Moses commanded, 35
which Joshua read not before all the assembly of Israel,
and the women, and the little ones, and the strangers that
were conversant among them.

ix. 1, 2. *The kings of Canaan unite against Joshua.*

These two verses form a general introduction to chs. ix.-xi. by
the editor.

And it came to pass, when all the kings which were 9
beyond Jordan, in the hill country, and in the lowland,
and on all the shore of the great sea in front of Lebanon,
the Hittite, and the Amorite, the Canaanite, the Perizzite,
the Hivite, and the Jebusite, heard thereof; that they 2
gathered themselves together, to fight with Joshua and
with Israel, with one accord.

3-15. *By a wile the Gibeonites obtain an alliance with Israel.*

The story of the Gibeonites circulated in more than one
form. Their request for a covenant is dealt with by "the men
of Israel" (*vv.* 6 *b*, 7; cf. x. 1); their offer of submission comes
before Joshua (*vv.* 8-11 *a*). The combination of accounts is seen
in the fact that the alliance is made and yet the Gibeonites are

---

34. afterward] i.e. after blessing.
the blessing and the curse] i.e. Dt. xxviii.
35. were conversant] marg. "Heb. *walked*." Cf. 1 S. xxv. 15.
The original meaning of the English word is "to live, or associate,
with."
ix. 1. the hill country] i.e. the central range of high hills.
the lowland] Heb. *shephēlah*, the region of lower hills that
lay between the central range and the sea coast.
heard thereof] Heb. *heard*. The object to the verb is
evidently that given in *v.* 3 (cf. x. 1) The omission of it shows
that the section viii. 30-35 is a later insertion; for when ix. 1
followed immediately on viii. 29 (as it does in LXX) the meaning
was clear without the addition of a definite object. See also xi. 1.

content to do slaves' work. *vv.* 17-21 are from a later form than either of the above.

Gibeon, which lay about six miles S.W. from Ai and a night's march from Gilgal (x. 9), was the head of three confederate cities (*v.* 17), and of some importance (x. 2), though apparently not governed by a king (*v.* 11). According to 2 S. xxi. 1, 2, the Gibeonites were independent as late as the time of David; and the present story, or at least one form of it, is an attempt to account for the remarkable fact that these Canaanite cities had for so long retained their independence in the very heart of Israelite territory. Some change must have taken place soon after the event recorded in 2 S. xxi., for in the first year of his reign Solomon "went to Gibeon to sacrifice there...In Gibeon the Lord appeared to Solomon" (1 K. iii. 4, 5). Perhaps the Gibeonites became incorporated with Israel (cf. Neh. iii. 7, vii. 25, where they are named amongst the returning exiles); but *vv.* 21-27 point to a tradition that they became servants of the Temple (cf. 1 K. ix. 20, 21).

3 But when the inhabitants of Gibeon heard what Joshua
4 had done unto Jericho and to Ai, they also did work wilily, and went and made as if they had been ambassadors, and took old sacks upon their asses, and wine-
5 skins, old and rent and bound up; and old shoes and clouted upon their feet, and old garments upon them; and all the bread of their provision was dry and was
6 become mouldy. And they went to Joshua unto the camp at Gilgal, and said unto him, and to the men of

---

4. they also] as well as the Israelites. We are not told expressly of any stratagem in connexion with the capture of Jericho.

wilily] "Wile" (="trick") is the same as "guile." The verb "beguile" (="to play a trick") occurs in *v.* 22. Cf. Numb. xxv. 18.

made as if etc.] Another meaning of the original word has been suggested—"they made themselves up." By the change of one letter the Heb. could mean "they took provisions" (so marg.).

wine-skins] The skins of goats were dried for the purpose of carrying liquids (wine, milk, water, 1 S. xvi. 20, Jud. iv. 19, Gen. xxi. 14). Cf. Mark ii. 22.

5. clouted]="patched."

mouldy] Heb. **crumbs** (so *v.* 12).

Israel, We are come from a far country : now therefore
make ye a covenant with us. And the men of Israel said 7
unto the Hivites, Peradventure ye dwell among us ; and
how shall we make a covenant with you ? And they said 8
unto Joshua, We are thy servants. And Joshua said unto
them, Who are ye ? and from whence come ye ? And 9
they said unto him, From a very far country thy servants
are come because of the name of the LORD thy God :
for we have heard the fame of him, and all that he did in
Egypt, and all that he did to the two kings of the Amorites, 10
that were beyond Jordan, to Sihon king of Heshbon, and
to Og king of Bashan, which was at Ashtaroth. And our 11
elders and all the inhabitants of our country spake to us,
saying, Take provision in your hand for the journey, and
go to meet them, and say unto them, We are your servants :
and now make ye a covenant with us. This our bread 12
we took hot for our provision out of our houses on the day
we came forth to go unto you ; but now, behold, it is dry,
and is become mouldy : and these wine-skins, which we 13
filled, were new ; and, behold, they be rent : and these
our garments and our shoes are become old by reason of
the very long journey. And the men took of their pro- 14
vision, and asked not counsel at the mouth of the LORD.
And Joshua made peace with them, and made a covenant 15

---

7. the Hivites] called in *v.* 3 *the inhabitants of Gibeon* (cf.
xi. 19).

9. the fame of him] Cf. vi. 27.

10. Cf. ii. 10. **Ashtaroth** was near to Edrei (xii. 4, xiii. 12).

11. and now make ye etc.] continues the account in *v.* 7.

14. the men] i.e. the men of Gibeon (x. 6). The fact that
the Heb. is plural, while for *the men of Israel* (*vv.* 6, 7) it is
sing., shows that the latter are not the subject. The Gibeonites
draw out of their sacks the dried bread as a proof of their asser-
tion.

and asked not etc.] This seems to have no connexion with
the first half of the verse. The subject must be the Israelites, who
did not seek Divine guidance in their perplexity (cf. 2 S. xxi. 1).

with them, to let them live : and the princes of the congregation sware unto them.

16–27.   *On being discovered the Gibeonites are condemned to menial work.*

16 And it came to pass at the end of three days after they
had made a covenant with them, that they heard that
they were their neighbours, and that they dwelt among
17 them.   And the children of Israel journeyed, and came
unto their cities on the third day.   Now their cities were
Gibeon, and Chephirah, and Beeroth, and Kiriath-jearim.
18 And the children of Israel smote them not, because the
princes of the congregation had sworn unto them by the
LORD, the God of Israel.   And all the congregation mur-
19 mured against the princes.   But all the princes said unto
all the congregation, We have sworn unto them by the
LORD, the God of Israel : now therefore we may not touch
20 them.   This we will do to them, and let them live ; lest
wrath be upon us, because of the oath which we sware unto
21 them.   And the princes said unto them, Let them live : so
they became hewers of wood and drawers of water unto all
the congregation ; as the princes had spoken unto them.
22 And Joshua called for them, and he spake unto them, saying, Wherefore have ye beguiled us, saying, We are very
23 far from you ; when ye dwell among us ?   Now therefore ye

---

the princes of the congregation] a characteristic phrase of the
late Priestly writer.
   17.   **Chephirah** (xviii. 26), **Beeroth** (xviii. 25), **Kiriath-jearim**
(xv. 9, 60)]   The first two were in Benjamin, the last in Judah.
   20.   **This**] described in *v.* 21.
   wrath]   The anger of God is thought of as having almost an
independent existence.   See Ex. xv. 7, Num. i. 53, xvi. 46.
   The famine in David's time (2 S. xxi. 1) was believed to be the
wrath of God visited upon Israel because Saul had broken the
oath made to the Gibeonites.
   22, 23 continue *v.* 16.

are cursed, and there shall never fail to be of you bond-men, both hewers of wood and drawers of water for the house of my God. And they answered Joshua, and said, 24 Because it was certainly told thy servants, how that the LORD thy God commanded his servant Moses to give you all the land, and to destroy all the inhabitants of the land from before you ; therefore we were sore afraid for our lives because of you, and have done this thing. And now, 25 behold, we are in thine hand : as it seemeth good and right unto thee to do unto us, do. And so did he unto 26 them, and delivered them out of the hand of the children of Israel, that they slew them not. And Joshua made 27 them that day hewers of wood and drawers of water for the congregation, and for the altar of the LORD, unto this day, in the place which he should choose.

x. 1–11. *The defeat of five kings of Southern Canaan.*

The following points will serve to elucidate the account of the battle of Gibeon, given in these verses :—

1. The distance from Gilgal to Gibeon is 18 miles, due W.

2. There is an Upper Beth-horon and a Nether (Lower) Beth-horon (xvi. 3, 5). Upper Beth-horon is 5 miles N.W. from Gibeon, and Nether Beth-horon is 2 miles W.N.W. from the Upper village. "Between the two places was a pass...leading from the region of Gibeon (el-Jîb) down to the western plain" (Robinson, *Biblical Researches*, 1856, II. p. 251). This pass is called, from the point of view of the Nether village, **the ascent of Beth-horon** (*v.* 10), and from that of the Upper village **the going down of Beth-horon** (*v.* 11 ; cf. vii. 5). Cf. 1 Macc. iii. 16, 24.

3. Neither Azēkah nor Makkēdah has been identified for certain ; but both places are said (xv. 35, 41) to be in the She-phēlah of Judah, i.e. in a S.W. direction from Gibeon.

4. The cities of the confederate kings lay to the S. of Gibeon : Jerusalem 5 miles, and Hebron 22 miles, both due S.; Jarmuth 16, Eglon 33, and Lachish 34, all S.W.

---

23. for the house etc.] Cf. *v.* 27, vi. 19, 24. Such servants of the Temple were called "the Nethinim, and the children of Solomon's servants" (Neh. vii. 60).

27. in the place etc.] A favourite Deuteronomic expression (Dt. xii. 5 etc. and xvi. 2 etc.).

It will be noticed that the enemy was first driven in a N.W.
direction and then to S.W. As this seems very improbable, it
has been thought that we have in this chapter, as elsewhere, a
combination of accounts. In one, Joshua who had to make the
forced march of 18 miles from Gilgal before he came up with the
enemy, drives them 6 or 7 miles further, by way of Beth-horon.
Their destruction is then completed by Divine interposition (the
hailstorm). In the other, the flight of the enemy to the S.W.
throws heavier work upon the Israelites ; but the writer probably
thought of them as marching from Ai, which was only 6 miles
distant from Gibeon.

This chapter forms a parallel to the story in Judg. i. 3-11.

10   Now it came to pass, when Adoni-zedek king of Jeru-
      salem heard how Joshua had taken Ai, and had utterly
      destroyed it ; as he had done to Jericho and her king, so
      he had done to Ai and her king ; and how the inhabitants
      of Gibeon had made peace with Israel, and were among
2   them ; that they feared greatly, because Gibeon was a
      great city, as one of the royal cities, and because it was
      greater than Ai, and all the men thereof were mighty.
3   Wherefore Adoni-zedek king of Jerusalem sent unto
      Hoham king of Hebron, and unto Piram king of Jarmuth,
      and unto Japhia king of Lachish, and unto Debir king of
4   Eglon, saying, Come up unto me, and help me, and let us
      smite Gibeon : for it hath made peace with Joshua and
5   with the children of Israel. Therefore the five kings of

---

x. 1. Adoni-zedek] means "Zedek [a Phoenician god] is
lord" (cf. Melchizedek, Gen. xiv. 18).

Jerusalem] The meaning of the word is uncertain, but the
city was called by this name before the Israelites entered Canaan.
The Amarna Letters (see p. xv) mention it as Urusalim.
Another name was Jebus (Jud. xix. 10), derived perhaps from its
Jebusite inhabitants (cf. xv. 8, xviii. 16, 28), but when the
Jebusites took possession of it is quite unknown. The city was
not taken on the present occasion (xv. 63, Jud. i. 21); indeed,
the Israelite history of Jerusalem only commences with the conquest of the fortress of Zion in the time of David (2 S. v. 6-9).

2. they feared] The subject is *Adoni-zedek*, and we must
read he feared.

3. Hebron] See on xiv. 15. **Lachish**] See on *v.* 31.

the Amorites, the king of Jerusalem, the king of Hebron,
the king of Jarmuth, the king of Lachish, the king of
Eglon, gathered themselves together, and went up, they
and all their hosts, and encamped against Gibeon, and
made war against it.   And the men of Gibeon sent unto 6
Joshua to the camp to Gilgal, saying, Slack not thy hand
from thy servants ; come up to us quickly, and save us,
and help us : for all the kings of the Amorites that dwell
in the hill country are gathered together against us.   So 7
Joshua went up from Gilgal, he, and all the people of war
with him, and all the mighty men of valour.   And the 8
LORD said unto Joshua, Fear them not : for I have
delivered them into thine hands ; there shall not a man
of them stand before thee.   Joshua therefore came upon 9
them suddenly ; *for* he went up from Gilgal all the night.
And the LORD discomfited them before Israel, and he 10
slew them with a great slaughter at Gibeon, and chased
them by the way of the ascent of Beth-horon, and smote
them to Azekah, and unto Makkedah.   And it came to 11
pass, as they fled from before Israel, while they were in
the going down of Beth-horon, that the LORD cast down
great stones from heaven upon them unto Azekah, and
they died : they were more which died with the hailstones
than they whom the children of Israel slew with the
sword.

---

6. **in the hill country**]   See on ix. 1.   Of the five cities
mentioned three (Jarmuth, Lachish, Eglon) were in the Shephēlah.

10. **discomfited**]   The word means lit. "to put out of order,"
so "to rout, to defeat."   Cf. Ex. xxiii. 27, Dt. vii. 23.

11. **unto Azekah**]   This must be an addition by the editor
who combined the two accounts of the flight.

great stones] i.e. **the hailstones.**   Cf. Ex. ix. 23, 24, Is. xxx.
30.

12–15. Joshua's prayer, and its answer.

12   Then spake Joshua to the LORD in the day when the
LORD delivered up the Amorites before the children of
Israel ; and he said in the sight of Israel,

> Sun, stand thou still upon Gibeon ;
> And thou, Moon, in the valley of Aijalon.

13   And the sun stood still, and the moon stayed,
> Until the nation had avenged themselves of their
> enemies.

Is not this written in the book of Jashar? And the sun
stayed in the midst of heaven, and hasted not to go down
14   about a whole day. And there was no day like that
before it or after it, that the LORD hearkened unto the
voice of a man : for the LORD fought for Israel.

15   And Joshua returned, and all Israel with him, unto the
camp to Gilgal.

---

12. Joshua sees a long day's work before him and prays that he
may be enabled to finish it before sunset.

Then spake Joshua to the LORD] An introduction by an
editor to the poetical quotation that follows, by which the
" standing still " of the sun is made to appear less a mighty act
of Joshua's than a fulfilment of a prayer addressed by him to
Jehovah.

stand thou still] marg. "Heb. *be silent.*" So *v.* 13.

The only time when a person from Beth-horon could see the
sun and the moon in the positions mentioned would be in the
early morning, the sun, of course, rising, and the moon setting.

13.   And the sun etc.] These words, which simply describe
the result of Joshua's command or prayer, do not form part of
the poem. They are probably a gloss upon the words "And the
sun stayed...," which has become misplaced.

Until the nation etc.] Rather, **Until the nation shall have
avenged themselves of their enemies.**

the book of Jashar] Apparently a collection of odes in praise
of the past deeds of Israel's heroes (cf. 2 S. i. 18). **Jashar**
means "upright."

in the midst of heaven] This forms part of the writer's inter-
pretation of the poem. He pictured the sun as remaining
motionless at mid-day.

14.   the LORD fought] Cf. *v.* 42, xxiii. 3, 10, Ex. xiv. 14, 24.

15. This verse (=*v.* 43) probably closed the account which

16-27.   *The capture and slaughter of the five kings.*

And these five kings fled, and hid themselves in the 16
cave at Makkedah.   And it was told Joshua, saying, The 17
five kings are found, hidden in the cave at Makkedah.
And Joshua said, Roll great stones unto the mouth of the 18
cave, and set men by it for to keep them : but stay not 19
ye ; pursue after your enemies, and smite the hindmost of
them ; suffer them not to enter into their cities : for the
LORD your God hath delivered them into your hand.
And it came to pass, when Joshua and the children of 20
Israel had made an end of slaying them with a very great
slaughter, till they were consumed, and the remnant which
remained of them had entered into the fenced cities, that 21
all the people returned to the camp to Joshua at Makkedah in peace : none moved his tongue against any of the
children of Israel.   Then said Joshua, Open the mouth of 22
the cave, and bring forth those five kings unto me out of
the cave.   And they did so, and brought forth those five 23
kings unto him out of the cave, the king of Jerusalem, the
king of Hebron, the king of Jarmuth, the king of Lachish,
the king of Eglon.   And it came to pass, when they 24
brought forth those kings unto Joshua, that Joshua called
for all the men of Israel, and said unto the chiefs of the
men of war which went with him, Come near, put your
feet upon the necks of these kings.   And they came near,

---

described the flight of the kings past Beth-horon, and should
follow *v.* 11.   The account of the flight to the S. W. is continued
in the next verse.

21.   to the camp to Joshua] These words can hardly be
original.   It is not likely that there was a camp at Makkedah,
and Joshua himself had (*v.* 20) joined in the pursuit.   The LXX
omits **to the camp.**

none moved his tongue etc.] i.e. no one said a word against
them ; no one annoyed them.   Cf. Ps. lxiv. 3 ; and Ex. xi. 7,
Judith xi. 19.

moved] marg. "Heb. *whetted*" (i.e. sharpened).

25 and put their feet upon the necks of them. And Joshua
said unto them, Fear not, nor be dismayed ; be strong
and of good courage : for thus shall the LORD do to all
26 your enemies against whom ye fight. And afterward
Joshua smote them, and put them to death, and hanged
them on five trees : and they were hanging upon the trees
27 until the evening. And it came to pass at the time of the
going down of the sun, that Joshua commanded, and they
took them down off the trees, and cast them into the cave
wherein they had hidden themselves, and laid great stones
on the mouth of the cave, unto this very day.

28-39. *The devoting of the cities of Makkedah, Libnah, Lachish, Eglon, Hebron, and Debir.*

Two things will be noticed about these verses, which are to a
large extent the work of a Deuteronomic editor :—*the statement*
that the conquests here described were achieved by " Joshua and
all Israel with him," and *the impression* that the cities fell one
after another in rapid succession (cf. xi. 10-15). See Introd. p. ix.

28 And Joshua took Makkedah on that day, and smote it
with the edge of the sword, and the king thereof ; he
utterly destroyed them and all the souls that were therein,
he left none remaining : and he did to the king of Makkedah as he had done unto the king of Jericho.

29 And Joshua passed from Makkedah, and all Israel with
30 him, unto Libnah, and fought against Libnah : and the
LORD delivered it also, and the king thereof, into the hand
of Israel ; and he smote it with the edge of the sword,
and all the souls that were therein ; he left none remaining in it ; and he did unto the king thereof as he had
done unto the king of Jericho.

---

27. unto this very day] Stones, believed to be those placed
by Joshua, were to be seen in the days of the writer. Cf. iv. 9.

29. Libnah] The site is not known, but according to xv. 42
it was in the Shephēlah of Judah. ˙

And Joshua passed from Libnah, and all Israel with 31
him, unto Lachish, and encamped against it, and fought
against it : and the LORD delivered Lachish into the hand 32
of Israel, and he took it on the second day, and smote it
with the edge of the sword, and all the souls that were
therein, according to all that he had done to Libnah.

Then Horam king of Gezer came up to help Lachish ; 33
and Joshua smote him and his people, until he had left
him none remaining.

And Joshua passed from Lachish, and all Israel with 34
him, unto Eglon ; and they encamped against it, and
fought against it ; and they took it on that day, and 35
smote it with the edge of the sword, and all the souls
that were therein he utterly destroyed that day, according
to all that he had done to Lachish.

And Joshua went up from Eglon, and all Israel with 36
him, unto Hebron ; and they fought against it : and they 37
took it, and smote it with the edge of the sword, and the
king thereof, and all the cities thereof, and all the souls
that were therein ; he left none remaining, according to
all that he had done to Eglon ; but he utterly destroyed
it, and all the souls that were therein.

And Joshua returned, and all Israel with him, to Debir ; 38

---

31. Lachish] an important place in the Shephēlah (xv. 39),
the modern *tell el-Hesy*. It was the first city in Palestine to be
excavated scientifically (1890), and the ruins of no less than
eleven cities have been discovered, built one over another and
ranging in date from B.C. 1700 to B.C. 400 (Driver, *Modern
Research*, pp. 41–46).

33. Gezer] a town, bordering on the Philistine country, 24
miles N.E. of Lachish. Its history goes back to an earlier stage
than that of Lachish, as neolithic remains have been found.
Joshua did not take Gezer (xvi. 10), and it remained Canaanite
till the time of Solomon (1 K. ix. 16).

37. the king thereof] Another account has already (*vv.* 23–
27) described his death.

38. returned] We should have expected that Joshua would
have taken Debir on his way to Hebron. As it is, the narrative

39 and fought against it : and he took it, and the king thereof, and all the cities thereof; and they smote them with
the edge of the sword, and utterly destroyed all the souls
that were therein ; he left none remaining : as he had
done to Hebron, so he did to Debir, and to the king
thereof; as he had done also to Libnah, and to the king
thereof.

40–43. *General summary of Israelite conquests in Southern Canaan.*

40 So Joshua smote all the land, the hill country, and the
South, and the lowland, and the slopes, and all their
kings ; he left none remaining : but he utterly destroyed
all that breathed, as the LORD, the God of Israel, com-
41 manded. And Joshua smote them from Kadesh-barnea
even unto Gaza, and all the country of Goshen, even unto
42 Gibeon. And all these kings and their land did Joshua
take at one time, because the LORD, the God of Israel,
43 fought for Israel. And Joshua returned, and all Israel
with him, unto the camp to Gilgal.

---

brings him " and all Israel with him " back again, and leaves them
in the S. W. of the Judaean mountains.

Debir] possibly a place 12 miles S. W. of Hebron.   See also on
xv. 15.

The editor has omitted the account of the capture of Jarmuth
(xii. 11).

40. the South] Heb. *negeb*, which means "the dry, or barren
land," is the term used of the most southerly portion of Canaan
before the actual desert is reached.

the slopes] i.e. the parts of the mountain range which fall
away towards the plains.   Cf. xii. 3, 8, xv. 46.

41. Kadesh-barnea] *'Ain Ḳadish*, 50 miles due S. of Beer-
sheba.

Gaza] A Philistine city, near the sea coast, 16 miles W. S. W.
of Lachish, never conquered by Israel (cf. xi. 22).

the country of Goshen] So xi. 16 ; and in xv. 51 a town of
Goshen is mentioned ; but nothing is known of either a country
or a town of this name in Palestine.   Contrast Gen. xlvi. 28.

Gibeon marks the N. limit, Kadesh-barnea the S., and Gaza
the W., of the land conquered by Israel up to this time.

xi. 1–9. *The defeat of the allied kings of Northern Canaan.*

In these verses we have a story parallel to that in Jud. iv. 2, 3, 23, 24. (Cf. ch. x. = Jud. i. 3–11.)

And it came to pass, when Jabin king of Hazor heard **11** thereof, that he sent to Jobab king of Madon, and to the king of Shimron, and to the king of Achshaph, and to the **2** kings that were on the north, in the hill country, and in the Arabah south of Chinneroth, and in the lowland, and in the heights of Dor on the west, to the Canaanite on **3** the east and on the west, and the Amorite, and the Hittite, and the Perizzite, and the Jebusite in the hill country, and the Hivite under Hermon in the land of Mizpah. And **4** they went out, they and all their hosts with them, much people, even as the sand that is upon the sea shore in multitude, with horses and chariots very many. And all **5** these kings met together; and they came and pitched together at the waters of Merom, to fight with Israel. And the LORD said unto Joshua, Be not afraid because of **6**

---

xi. 1. Hazor] Site not known, but said (xix. 36) to be in Naphtali.

Of the other three towns nothing is known for certain. The last two are mentioned later (xix. 15, 25).

2–4. A Deuteronomic expansion.

2. The site of **Chinneroth** (*Chinnereth*, xix. 35) has not been determined, but it gave its name to the *sea of Chinneroth* (xii. 3, xiii. 27), called in later times the Lake of Gennesaret (Luke v. 1), or Sea of Galilee (Matt. iv. 18).

the heights of Dor] marg. "Or, *Naphoth Dor.*" Cf. xii. 23, xvii. 11, 1 K. iv. 11. **Dor** is supposed to be the present *Tanturah*, a maritime city, about 10 miles N. of Caesarea; **the heights of Dor** are the W. and S.W. slopes of Carmel.

3. Mizpah] also Mizpeh (= watch tower), a name of frequent occurrence. The **land of Mizpah** is perhaps the country stretching S. from Hermon toward Lake Ḥūleh.

4. chariots] See Introd. p. xvii.

5. met] **agreed**, Amos iii. 3. This verse continues *v.* 1.

Merom] thought to be a place in the plain that lies some few miles N. of Dothan. The allied kings, therefore, move south to meet Joshua.

them : for to-morrow at this time will I deliver them up
all slain before Israel : thou shalt hough their horses,
7 and burn their chariots with fire. So Joshua came, and
all the people of war with him, against them by the waters
8 of Merom suddenly, and fell upon them. And the LORD
delivered them into the hand of Israel, and they smote
them, and chased them unto great Zidon, and unto Misrephoth-maim, and unto the valley of Mizpeh eastward ;
and they smote them, until they left them none remaining.
9 And Joshua did unto them as the LORD bade him : he
houghed their horses, and burnt their chariots with fire.

10-15. *The devoting of their cities.*

These verses are a Deuteronomic review of the Northern
campaign. Cf. x. 28–43, of the Southern.

10   And Joshua turned back at that time, and took Hazor,
and smote the king thereof with the sword : for Hazor
11 beforetime was the head of all those kingdoms. And
they smote all the souls that were therein with the edge
of the sword, utterly destroying them : there was none
12 left that breathed : and he burnt Hazor with fire. And
all the cities of those kings, and all the kings of them, did
Joshua take, and he smote them with the edge of the
sword, and utterly destroyed them ; as Moses the servant
13 of the LORD commanded. But as for the cities that stood
on their mounds, Israel burned none of them, save Hazor

---

6. hough] Pronounce **hock**, to cut " the joint in the hind-
leg of an animal, between knee and fetlock " (Skeat).   2 S.
viii. 4.
8.   The hostile army is broken up, and part is driven N.W.
and part E.
13.   their mounds] i.e. heaps, formed by the ruins of previous
cities (see on x. 31).   For the word *těl* (= " heap ") see viii. 28,
Dt. xiii. 16, Jer. xxx. 18, xlix. 2, and cf. the common designation
of places in the East, e.g. Tel-abib, Ezek. iii. 15, tell el-Hesy,
tell el-Amarna, etc.

only ; that did Joshua burn. And all the spoil of these 14
cities, and the cattle, the children of Israel took for a prey
unto themselves ; but every man they smote with the
edge of the sword, until they had destroyed them, neither
left they any that breathed. As the LORD commanded 15
Moses his servant, so did Moses command Joshua : and
so did Joshua ; he left nothing undone of all that the
LORD commanded Moses.

16-20. A summary of all the conquests of Joshua.

So Joshua took all that land, the hill country, and all 16
the South, and all the land of Goshen, and the lowland,
and the Arabah, and the hill country of Israel, and the
lowland of the same ; from mount Halak, that goeth up 17
to Seir, even unto Baal-gad in the valley of Lebanon
under mount Hermon : and all their kings he took, and
smote them, and put them to death. Joshua made war a 18
long time with all those kings. There was not a city that 19
made peace with the children of Israel, save the Hivites
the inhabitants of Gibeon : they took all in battle. For 20
it was of the LORD to harden their hearts, to come against
Israel in battle, that he might utterly destroy them, that
they might have no favour, but that he might destroy
them, as the LORD commanded Moses.

---

16. Cf. x. 40, 41.

the hill country] i.e. of Judah, contrasted (as *v.* 21) with the
hill country of Israel. Cf. xv. 48-60.

17.   mount Halak] marg. "Or, *the bare mountain*," so called
perhaps from the absence of vegetation. Cf. xii. 7.

Seir] the extensive range of mountains, lying outside Palestine,
to the south. It belonged to Edom, and was sometimes used
as a general name for Edomite territory (xxiv. 4, Dt. ii. 1-8).

Baal-gad] an unknown place in the extreme north (xii. 7,
xiii. 5).

18.   a long time] Heb. *many days* (as xxii. 3, xxiii. 1). On
the length of the conquest see Introd. pp. ix, xix.

20.   favour] i.e. favour shown by Jehovah (as Ezra ix. 8).

21-23.   The expulsion of the Anākim.   Concluding summary.

These verses are a late appendix.

21   And Joshua came at that time, and cut off the Anakim
from the hill country, from Hebron, from Debir, from
Anab, and from all the hill country of Judah, and from all
the hill country of Israel: Joshua utterly destroyed them
22 with their cities.   There was none of the Anakim left in
the land of the children of Israel: only in Gaza, in Gath,
23 and in Ashdod, did some remain.   So Joshua took the
whole land, according to all that the LORD spake unto
Moses; and Joshua gave it for an inheritance unto Israel
according to their divisions by their tribes.   And the land
had rest from war.

xii.   1-6.   The conquests east of the Jordan.

These verses, which recapitulate the narrative of Dt. ii. 26-iii. 17,
do not belong properly to the story of Joshua.   They were
inserted by the editor who desired to give a complete survey of
the land conquered and possessed by Israel.   In ch. xiii. the
country is described more fully.

12   Now these are the kings of the land, whom the children
of Israel smote, and possessed their land beyond Jordan
toward the sunrising, from the valley of Arnon unto
2 mount Hermon, and all the Arabah eastward: Sihon
king of the Amorites, who dwelt in Heshbon, and ruled

---

21.   Cf. x. 36-39, where the devoting of Hebron and Debir
has already been described.

The Anākim (lit. "long necked"), believed to be of gigantic
stature (Dt. ii. 10), lived in Hebron and were driven out by Caleb
(xiv. 13, xv. 13, 14, Jud. i. 20).   In this verse the expulsion is
attributed to Joshua.

Anab] xv. 50.   It lay about 13 miles S.W. of Hebron.

22.   Gaza...Gath...Ashdod] Philistine cities (xiii. 3).   See on
x. 41, xiii. 2, 3.

did some remain]   This statement allows for the appearance
in later times of Goliath of Gath.   Cf. 1 S. xvii. 4, 2 S. xxi. 19.

from Aroer, which is on the edge of the valley of Arnon,
and *the city that is in* the middle of the valley, and half
Gilead, even unto the river Jabbok, the border of the
children of Ammon; and the Arabah unto the sea of 3
Chinneroth, eastward, and unto the sea of the Arabah,
even the Salt Sea, eastward, the way to Beth-jeshimoth;
and on the south, under the slopes of Pisgah : and the 4
border of Og king of Bashan, of the remnant of the Rephaim, who dwelt at Ashtaroth and at Edrei, and ruled in 5
mount Hermon, and in Salecah, and in all Bashan, unto
the border of the Geshurites and the Maacathites, and half
Gilead, the border of Sihon king of Heshbon. Moses the 6
servant of the LORD and the children of Israel smote

---

xii. 1. The **Arnon** flows into the Dead Sea at a spot about
midway along the eastern shore.

2. the city that is etc.] an unknown place. See xiii. 9, 16,
Dt. ii. 36.

The land of Gilead (xvii. 6), or **Gilead** (xiii. 11), embraced in
its widest meaning all the East Jordan district (e.g. xxii. 9, Jud.
xx. 1). Sometimes, however, Bashan (see on *v.* 5) was not
included, and we find "the land of Gilead and Bashan" (xvii.
5, 2 K. x. 33; cf. Dt. iii. 12, 13). Gilead was divided by the
Jabbok into the southern half (as here, and *v.* 5) and the northern
half (xiii. 31).

3. Beth-jeshimoth lay about two miles E. of the northern end
of the Dead Sea. **Pisgah,** or Nebo (Dt. xxxiv. 1), is one of the
mountains of Abārim (Num. xxxiii. 47), a range situated at the
N.E. of the Dead Sea. The **slopes of Pisgah** (cf. x. 40) mean
those parts of the mountain which fall away towards the Dead
Sea.

4. The **Rephāim,** like the Anākim (xi. 21), were believed
to be giants (Dt. ii. 11, 20, iii. 11); their land is mentioned in
xvii. 15.

who dwelt] The subject is **Og**.

Edrei] almost due E. of the southern end of the Sea of Galilee
and distant from it about 30 miles.

5. Salĕcah lay about 30 miles E.S.E. of Edrei.

Bashan] the country between the Yarmuk and Mt. Hermon.
Geshur and Maacah were petty Aramaean states, lying S. of
Mt. Hermon (cf. xiii. 11). The *Geshurites* of xiii. 2 and 1 S.
xxvii. 8 are a different people.

them : and Moses the servant of the LORD gave it for a possession unto the Reubenites, and the Gadites, and the half tribe of Manasseh.

7–24.   *The conquests west of the Jordan.*

7   And these are the kings of the land whom Joshua and the children of Israel smote beyond Jordan westward, from Baal-gad in the valley of Lebanon even unto mount Halak, that goeth up to Seir ; and Joshua gave it unto the tribes of Israel for a possession according to their 8 divisions ; in the hill country, and in the lowland, and in the Arabah, and in the slopes, and in the wilderness, and in the South ; the Hittite, the Amorite, and the Canaanite, 9 the Perizzite, the Hivite, and the Jebusite : the king of Jericho, one ; the king of Ai, which is beside Beth-el, 10 one ; the king of Jerusalem, one ; the king of Hebron, 11 one ; the king of Jarmuth, one ; the king of Lachish, 12 one ; the king of Eglon, one ; the king of Gezer, one ; the 13 14 king of Debir, one ; the king of Geder, one ; the king of 15 Hormah, one ; the king of Arad, one ; the king of Libnah, 16 one ; the king of Adullam, one ; the king of Makkedah, 17 one ; the king of Beth-el, one ; the king of Tappuah, one ; 18 the king of Hepher, one ; the king of Aphek, one ; the 19 king of Lassharon, one ; the king of Madon, one ; the 20 king of Hazor, one ; the king of Shimron-meron, one ; 21 the king of Achshaph, one ; the king of Taanach, one ; 22 the king of Megiddo, one ; the king of Kedesh, one ; the 23 king of Jokneam in Carmel, one ; the king of Dor in the

---

7, 8.   See xi. 16, 17, and iii. 10.

8.   the wilderness] i.e. of Judah (xv. 61).

9–24.   This list contains 14 place-names not hitherto mentioned.

18.   Read (partly with LXX) **the king of Aphek in Sharon.** *Sharon* is a fertile plain in the Philistine country bordering on the coast between Joppa and Dor.   **Aphek** (xix. 30) is not the Aphek of xiii. 4.

height of Dor, one ; the king of Goiim in Gilgal, one ; the 24 king of Tirzah, one : all the kings thirty and one.

PART II.   CHAPTERS XIII–XXI.

THE ALLOTMENT OF THE LAND.

xiii. 1-7. Joshua's instructions for the allotment of the unconquered land.

The opening verses of this chapter originally dealt with the allotment of the land of Canaan among the tribes in the closing years of Joshua's life. The original version can be read in *vv.* 1 and 7, followed by xviii. 2–10, and this should be compared with a parallel account by a late writer in xiv. 1–5. The Deuteronomic editor misunderstood the meaning of **very much land** (*v.* 1) ; and instead of making it refer to the land of Canaan which had been conquered but not occupied, he interpreted it of the land belonging chiefly to the Philistines and Phoenicians, which lay outside the proper limits of Israelite territory, and by inserting *vv.* 2-6 gave an entirely different complexion to the narrative.

Now Joshua was old and well stricken in years ; and 13 the LORD said unto him, Thou art old and well stricken in years, and there remaineth yet very much land to be possessed. This is the land that yet remaineth : all the 2 regions of the Philistines, and all the Geshurites ; from 3

---

23. Read **the king of nations in Galilee** (cf. Is. ix. 1). The LXX has Galilee for **Gilgal**, and **Goiim** is the Heb. for *nations* (cf. marg. and Jud. iv. 2).

24. thirty and one] The correction in *v.* 18 reduces the total to 30. LXX has 29, but shows variations from the Heb.

xiii. 1. well stricken in years] Heb. "gone [i.e. advanced] in years." According to xxiv. 29 Joshua was 110 when he died.

stricken, formerly spelt "striken," ptc. of "to strike," which originally meant "to proceed, advance."

2-6. Cf. Jud. iii. 3.

2. The Philistines are first mentioned among the peoples who, coming both by land and sea from the S.W. of Asia Minor and the Aegean Isles, threatened the Egyptian kingdom *c.* B.C. 1200. With this agrees the tradition (Dt. ii. 23 ; cf. Amos ix. 7) which calls them *Caphtorim*, as coming from Caphtor (probably Crete). They settled on the coast-land S. of Joppa, the district being called after them Pelesheth (Ex. xv. 14). But this name was used by the Greeks to denote the whole of Canaan ; hence

the Shihor, which is before Egypt, even unto the border
of Ekron northward, *which* is counted to the Canaanites ;
the five lords of the Philistines ; the Gazites, and the
Ashdodites, the Ashkelonites, the Gittites, and the Ek-
4 ronites ; also the Avvim, on the south : all the land of the
Canaanites, and Mearah that belongeth to the Zidonians,
5 unto Aphek, to the border of the Amorites : and the land
of the Gebalites, and all Lebanon, toward the sunrising,
from Baal-gad under mount Hermon unto the entering in
6 of Hamath : all the inhabitants of the hill country from

Palestine.   Their   principal   towns   are   mentioned   in   *v.*   3.
Some tombs, recently discovered at Gezer, are "really the first
tangible remains of the Philistines that excavation has revealed "
(Macalister).

3.   the Shihor] i.e. "the black " (from the colour of its mud
deposit), a name for the Nile (cf. Is. xxiii. 3, Jer. ii. 18).   The
most easterly arm of the Nile is meant.   Cf. 1 Ch. xiii. 5.

which **is counted**...] The subject must be **the land** (*v.* 2).

Ekron was the most northerly of the five cities and was famous
for its worship of Baal-zebub (2 K. i. 2), and *Gaza* (see on x. 41)
the most southerly, while *Ashdod* (xi. 22), the most important of
the five, and *Ashkelon*, the only maritime city, lay between the
two.   The site of *Gath* (xi. 22) is uncertain, but it seems to have
lain nearest to the territory of Judah, and it was the only one
that was conquered by Israel (1 Ch. xviii. 1 = 2 S. viii. 1).   It is
omitted in the list of Amos (i. 6–8).

4.   also the Avvim, on the south] This concludes the description of the southern peoples.   In the rest of this verse and
in *v.* 5 the northern peoples are named.

Avvim] apparently a remnant of the people said to have been
destroyed in Dt. ii. 23.

the land of the Canaanites] i.e. Phoenicia (Dt. i. 7).

and Mearah] The reading *from Mearah* has been suggested.
Mearah = "a cave " and may refer to a grotto, situated just N.
of Tyre, which was famed for the worship of the goddess Astarte.

Zidonians] not merely the inhabitants of Zidon (xi. 8), but
Phoenicians generally (1 K. v. 6).

Aphek] N.E. of Beirût : the modern *Afka*.

5.   Gebalites] Gebel or Gebal (Ps. lxxxiii. 7, Ezek. xxvii. 9)
lay on the Phoenician coast and was a centre of the worship of
Adonis.   The Greeks called it Byblos.

the entering in of Hamath] a stereotyped phrase for the
northern border of Israelite territory : Num. xiii. 21, xxxiv. 8,

Lebanon unto Misrephoth-maim, even all the Zidonians ; them will I drive out from before the children of Israel : only allot thou it unto Israel for an inheritance, as I have commanded thee. Now therefore divide this land for an 7 inheritance unto the nine tribes, and the half tribe of Manasseh.

8-13. *The inheritances of the trans-Jordanic tribes summarized.*

See notes on xii. 1-6.

With him the Reubenites and the Gadites received 8 their inheritance, which Moses gave them, beyond Jordan eastward, even as Moses the servant of the LORD gave them ; from Aroer, that is on the edge of 9 the valley of Arnon, and the city that is in the middle of the valley, and all the plain of Medeba unto Dibon ; and 10 all the cities of Sihon king of the Amorites, which reigned in Heshbon, unto the border of the children of Ammon ; and Gilead, and the border of the Geshurites and Maacath- 11 ites, and all mount Hermon, and all Bashan unto Salecah ; all the kingdom of Og in Bashan, which reigned in Ash- 12

---

1 K. viii. 65, Amos vi. 14. **Hamath**, an important Hittite city, was on the Orontes, and by **the entering in of Hamath** is probably meant the pass between Hermon and Lebanon by which N. Syria is approached, but this is fully 120 miles south of the city.

6. them will I etc.] **I will drive them out.**

7. This verse, which should be connected with *v.* 1 and xviii. 2-10, read originally " Now therefore divide this land [i.e. the land of Canaan which had been conquered but not occupied] for an inheritance unto the seven tribes." The tribes which according to this writer had at the period mentioned (*v.* 1) received their inheritance were Reuben and Gad (E. of Jordan), Judah (xv.), and Joseph (= Ephraim and Manasseh, xvi. and xvii.). Levi (*v.* 14) had no allotment ; seven tribes, therefore, remained.

8. With him] i.e Eastern Manasseh, though the words seem to refer to the Western half, just named.

9. Medeba, a few miles south of Heshbon ; **Dibon**, north of the Arnon.

taroth and in Edrei (the same was left of the remnant of
the Rephaim); for these did Moses smite, and drave them
13 out.   Nevertheless the children of Israel drave not out
the Geshurites, nor the Maacathites: but Geshur and
Maacath dwelt in the midst of Israel, unto this day.

14. *Concerning the tribe of Levi.*

14 Only unto the tribe of Levi he gave none inheritance; the
offerings of the LORD, the God of Israel, made by fire are
his inheritance, as he spake unto him.

15-23. *The inheritance of Reuben.*

15   And Moses gave unto the tribe of the children of
16 Reuben according to their families.   And their border
was from Aroer, that is on the edge of the valley of
Arnon, and the city that is in the middle of the valley,
17 and all the plain by Medeba; Heshbon, and all her cities
that are in the plain; Dibon, and Bamoth-baal, and Beth-
18 baal-meon; and Jahaz, and Kedemoth, and Mephaath;
19 and Kiriathaim, and Sibmah, and Zereth-shahar in the
20 mount of the valley; and Beth-peor, and the slopes of Pis-
21 gah, and Beth-jeshimoth; and all the cities of the plain, and

---

12.   for these etc.] **and Moses smote them and drave them
out.**

13.   Nevertheless] **And.**   The verse has been incorporated by
the editor from an older source.

14.   Cf. *v.* 33, xviii. 7.

the offerings...made by fire]   Or, "fire-offerings."   The word
is an insertion, as appears from *v.* 33.

15.   And Moses gave]   These words commence an extract
(*vv.* 15-32) from the Priestly writer which describes, in fuller
detail than *vv.* 8-12, the inheritances of the tribes on the east of
Jordan.

19.   the mount of the valley]   The **mount** is Attārus, and the
valley must mean the flat open country to the W. and S.W. of
the mount.

20.   Beth-peor was close to the final encampment of Israel
(Dt. iii. 29).   See further on xxii. 17.

21.   See Num. xxxi. 8.

all the kingdom of Sihon king of the Amorites, which
reigned in Heshbon, whom Moses smote with the chiefs
of Midian, Evi, and Rekem, and Zur, and Hur, and Reba,
the princes of Sihon, that dwelt in the land.   Balaam also 22
the son of Beor, the soothsayer, did the children of Israel
slay with the sword among the rest of their slain.   And 23
the border of the children of Reuben was Jordan, and the
border *thereof*.   This was the inheritance of the children
of Reuben according to their families, the cities and the
villages thereof.

24-28. *The inheritance of Gad.*

And Moses gave unto the tribe of Gad, unto the 24
children of Gad, according to their families.   And their 25
border was Jazer, and all the cities of Gilead, and half
the land of the children of Ammon, unto Aroer that is
before Rabbah ; and from Heshbon unto Ramath-mizpeh, 26
and Betonim ; and from Mahanaim unto the border of
Debir ; and in the valley, Beth-haram, and Beth-nimrah, 27
and Succoth, and Zaphon, the rest of the kingdom of

---

22.   Balaam] Cf. xxiv. 9, 10, Num. xxii.–xxiv., xxxi. 8.

soothsayer] This English word meant originally "one who
says the truth " (cf. Num. xxii. 18 as regards Balaam), but it is
now used only of one who foretells events, a diviner.

23.   and the border thereof] **for a border**.   The phrase also
occurs *v*. 27, xv. 12, 47.

25.   all the cities of Gilead] But according to *v*. 31 " half
Gilead " was assigned to E. Manasseh.

Ammon] A Semitic people E. of the Jordan (Num. xxi. 24,
Dt. ii. 19).

Aroer] a different place from that mentioned in *v*. 16, and unknown.

26.   Heshbon] also mentioned in xxi. 39 as belonging to Gad.
Contrast *v*. 17.

Mahanaim] Reckoned to Eastern Manasseh in *v*. 30.   It was
a place of some importance, lying on the northern side of the
Jabbok (Gen. xxxii. 2, 21, 22, 2 S. ii. 8, 1 K. iv. 14).

Debir] Rather, as marg., **Lidebir** (perhaps=*Lo-debar*, 2 S.
ix. 4).

Sihon king of Heshbon, Jordan and the border *thereof*,
unto the uttermost part of the sea of Chinnereth beyond
28 Jordan eastward. This is the inheritance of the children
of Gad according to their families, the cities and the
villages thereof.

29–31. *The inheritance of Eastern Manasseh.*

29 And Moses gave *inheritance* unto the half tribe of
Manasseh : and it was for the half tribe of the children
30 of Manasseh according to their families. And their
border was from Mahanaim, all Bashan, all the kingdom
of Og king of Bashan, and all the towns of Jair, which
31 are in Bashan, threescore cities : and half Gilead, and
Ashtaroth, and Edrei, the cities of the kingdom of Og in
Bashan, were for the children of Machir the son of
Manasseh, even for the half of the children of Machir
according to their families.

32, 33. *Concluding summary of the inheritances on the east of Jordan.*

32 These are the inheritances which Moses distributed in
the plains of Moab, beyond the Jordan at Jericho, eastward.

---

27. uttermost part] Heb. **end** (i.e. the southern end) ; so
rendered in xv. 5. **Uttermost** (="outmost" or "utmost"), the
superlative of "out."

28. This is] **This was** (as *v.* 23).

29. And Moses gave] The tradition that the settlement of
half-Manasseh E. of the Jordan was the work of Moses (cf. also
v. 8, i. 12–14, xii. 6 etc.) differs from that referred to in xvii. 14–18
and Num. xxxii. 39, from which passages it appears that,
owing to the "one lot" which the Joseph tribes (Manasseh and
Ephraim) had received in Canaan from Joshua being insufficient
for their needs, they were forced to migrate to Gilead (the trans-
Jordanic country).

30. towns] Heb. *havvoth*, i.e. hamlets (of tents). Here, and
in Dt. iii. 14, these are placed in Bashan ; elsewhere (Num.
xxxii. 41) in Gilead. But see on xii. 2.

31. even for the half etc.] the other half being W. of the
Jordan.

32. the plains of Moab] So Num. xxii. 1 etc. The phrase

But unto the tribe of Levi Moses gave none inheritance : 33
the LORD, the God of Israel, is their inheritance, as he
spake unto them.

xiv. 1–5. *Introduction to the account of the allotment of the*
land west of the Jordan.

These verses, originally preceded by xviii. 1, form the introduction by the Priestly writer to the division of Western Canaan.
His account occupies the larger portion of chs. xv.–xxi.

And these are the inheritances which the children of **14**
Israel took in the land of Canaan, which Eleazar the
priest, and Joshua the son of Nun, and the heads of the
fathers' *houses* of the tribes of the children of Israel,
distributed unto them, by the lot of their inheritance, as 2
the LORD commanded by the hand of Moses, for the
nine tribes, and for the half tribe. For Moses had given 3
the inheritance of the two tribes and the half tribe beyond
Jordan : but unto the Levites he gave none inheritance
among them. For the children of Joseph were two tribes, 4
Manasseh and Ephraim : and they gave no portion unto
the Levites in the land, save cities to dwell in, with the
suburbs thereof for their cattle and for their substance.
As the LORD commanded Moses, so the children of Israel 5
did, and they divided the land.

---

means that part of the Arābah which lies N. of the Dead Sea,
and E. of the Jordan, opposite Jericho (Num. xxxv. 1).

xiv. 1. Eleazar] Notice the prominent position assigned to
Eleazar the priest here and in xvii. 4, xix. 51, xxi. 1, and
contrast with xiii. 1, 7*a*, xiv. 6, xviii. 3, 9, 10, and i.–xii. *passim*,
where Joshua is the sole agent of Jehovah. For passages relating
to Eleazar see xxiv. 33, Num. xvi. 37–40, xx. 28, Dt. x. 6.

4. and they gave] i.e. (as in xxi. 3) the children of Israel
gave.

cities] Contrast *v*. 3, xiii. 14, 33 ; and see Introd. to ch. xxi.
suburbs] Better, as marg., **pasture lands.** So xxi. 2, 11.
cattle…substance] Cf. Gen. xxxiv. 23. **Substance** means
here " property."

6–15. Caleb asks for and receives Hebron as his inheritance.

These verses contain a Deuteronomic account of Caleb's inheritance, which is fuller (and later) than the account appearing in xv. 13–19, and are an attempt to explain how the important city of Hebron came into the possession of a non-Israelite.

6 Then the children of Judah drew nigh unto Joshua in Gilgal: and Caleb the son of Jephunneh the Kenizzite said unto him, Thou knowest the thing that the LORD spake unto Moses the man of God concerning me and 7 concerning thee in Kadesh-barnea. Forty years old was I when Moses the servant of the LORD sent me from Kadesh-barnea to spy out the land; and I brought him 8 word again as it was in mine heart. Nevertheless my brethren that went up with me made the heart of the people melt: but I wholly followed the LORD my God. 9 And Moses sware on that day, saying, Surely the land whereon thy foot hath trodden shall be an inheritance to thee and to thy children for ever, because thou hast 10 wholly followed the LORD my God. And now, behold, the LORD hath kept me alive, as he spake, these forty

---

6. Gilgal] According to this editor, Gilgal is still the national centre (cf. on viii. 3).

The Kenizzites were an Edomite people (cf. xv. 17 and Gen. xxxvi. 8–11) who seem to have lived in S. Palestine and eventually to have become merged in Judah; hence Caleb in the later tradition is called a Judaean (Num. xiii. 6), and Hebron in xv. 54 is reckoned to Judah.

the thing etc.] Num. xiv. 24, 30.

and concerning thee] An early tradition (Num. xiii. 30, xiv. 24; cf. Dt. i. 36) does not mention Joshua as one of the spies. The words, too, **my brethren** (*v.* 8) and **thou heardest** etc. (*v.* 12) imply that Joshua was not with Caleb. If this be correct, the words **and concerning thee** must be an addition by a Priestly editor, to harmonize with the late Priestly tradition.

7. as it was etc.] These words imply not so much that his report was a true one according to his belief—the other spies might have made the same claim—as that he made it calmly and deliberately and in anticipation of the reception which would be accorded to it (Num. xiii. 30, 31, xiv. 6–10).

and five years, from the time that the LORD spake this word unto Moses, while Israel walked in the wilderness : and now, lo, I am this day fourscore and five years old. As yet I am as strong this day as I was in the day that 11 Moses sent me : as my strength was then, even so is my strength now, for war, and to go out and to come in. Now therefore give me this mountain, whereof the LORD 12 spake in that day ; for thou heardest in that day how the Anakim were there, and cities great and fenced : it may be that the LORD will be with me, and I shall drive them out, as the LORD spake. And Joshua blessed him ; and 13 he gave Hebron unto Caleb the son of Jephunneh for an inheritance. Therefore Hebron became the inheritance 14 of Caleb the son of Jephunneh the Kenizzite, unto this day ; because that he wholly followed the LORD, the God of Israel. Now the name of Hebron beforetime was 15 Kiriath-arba ; *which Arba was* the greatest man among the Anakim. And the land had rest from war.

---

10. these forty and five years] i.e. the 45 years between the return of the spies to Kadesh-barnea and the point now reached in the story, when the conquest of the land both E. and W. of Jordan is represented as being completed. This is the only place in *Joshua* which gives any information as to the length of time taken in the conquest. According as we make the wanderings in the wilderness last 38 years (Dt. ii. 14) or 40 years (Josh. v. 6, Num. xiv. 33, Dt. viii. 2, 4, Amos ii. 10) the length of the conquest will be 7 or 5 years. Cf. on xi. 18.

12. this mountain] The neighbourhood of Hebron is the highest in S. Palestine.

Another rendering of this verse is—"for thou heardest [what the LORD said] in that day. For the Anākim are there, and cities..." This agrees better with xv. 14.

15. Hebron lay about 18 miles S. of Jerusalem. The original name was Kiriath-arba (Gen. xxiii. 2), i.e. "the city of four," perhaps so called as being the city of four confederate chiefs. The Heb. for "four" is *arba*, and this was thought in later times to be the name of the founder of the city (xv. 13, xxi. 11). It is possible, however, that it is the name of a god. Previous notices have recorded the devoting of Hebron by Joshua (x. 37), and the expulsion of the Anākim from it (xi. 21).

xv. 1–12. *The inheritance of Judah delineated.*

These verses describe the line of territory which formed the
border of Judah : S. *vv.* 2–4 (cf. Num. xxxiv. 3–5), E. *v.* 5*a*,
N. *vv.* 5*b*—11, W. *v.* 12*a*. Some of the places are unknown,
and the identification of others is doubtful ; it is not possible
therefore to follow completely the description given.

15   And the lot for the tribe of the children of Judah
according to their families was unto the border of Edom,
even to the wilderness of Zin southward, at the uttermost
2 part of the south.   And their south border was from the
uttermost part of the Salt Sea, from the bay that looked
3 southward : and it went out southward of the ascent of
Akrabbim, and passed along to Zin, and went up by the
south of Kadesh-barnea, and passed along by Hezron,
4 and went up to Addar, and turned about to Karka : and
it passed along to Azmon, and went out at the brook of
Egypt ; and the goings out of the border were at the sea :
5 this shall be your south border.   And the east border
was the Salt Sea, even unto the end of Jordan.   And the
border of the north quarter was from the bay of the sea
6 at the end of Jordan : and the border went up to Beth-
hoglah, and passed along by the north of Beth-arabah ;
and the border went up to the stone of Bohan the son of
7 Reuben : and the border went up to Debir from the
valley of Achor, and so northward, looking toward Gilgal,

---

xv. 1.   the lot] i.e. the inheritance obtained by means of the
lot. So xvi. 1, xvii. 1.

3.   the ascent of Akrabbim] or, the Pass of Scorpions,
thought to be the modern *eṣ-Ṣafa*, on the road from Petra to
Hebron.   Num. xxxiv. 4

4.   the brook of Egypt] is the *Wādy el-'Arish*.

this shall be etc.]   A quotation from another source, as the
use of the second pers. pron. shows.

5 b–11. Cf. the southern border of Benjamin, as given in
xviii. 15–20.

6.   the stone of Bohan]   Some memorial stone (cf. 1 S. vii.
12, 2 S. xviii. 18).

7.   Debir] not the same place as that mentioned in *v.* **15.**

Gilgal] not the same as the Gilgal of xiv. 6.

that is over against the ascent of Adummim, which is on
the south side of the river : and the border passed along
to the waters of En-shemesh, and the goings out thereof
were at En-rogel : and the border went up by the valley 8
of the son of Hinnom unto the side of the Jebusite southward (the same is Jerusalem) : and the border went up
to the top of the mountain that lieth before the valley of
Hinnom westward, which is at the uttermost part of the
vale of Rephaim northward : and the border was drawn 9
from the top of the mountain unto the fountain of the
waters of Nephtoah, and went out to the cities of mount
Ephron ; and the border was drawn to Baalah (the same
is Kiriath-jearim) : and the border turned about from 10
Baalah westward unto mount Seir, and passed along unto
the side of mount Jearim on the north (the same is
Chesalon), and went down to Beth-shemesh, and passed
along by Timnah : and the border went out unto the side 11
of Ekron northward : and the border was drawn to Shik-
keron, and passed along to mount Baalah, and went out
at Jabneel ; and the goings out of the border were at the

---

8. the valley etc.] The valley W. and S. of Jerusalem,
notorious for the offering of human sacrifices (2 K. xxiii. 10).
As Gehenna (Mt. v. 22) it became a symbolical name for the
place of torment. It is called **the valley of Hinnom** in the latter
part of this verse and also in xviii. 16. Nothing is known of
Hinnom.

Jerusalem] x. 1. Here the city is outside the limits of Judah :
see on *v.* 63.

9. Nephtoah] supposed to be *Lifta*, about two miles N.W. of
Jerusalem. **Mount Ephron** is not known.

Kiriath-jearim] i.e. *city of forests* (or *copses*), evidently a
city connected with the worship of Baal (*v.* 60). See further ix.
17, Jud. xviii. 12, 1 S. vii. 1, 1 Ch. xiii. 5 (cf. Ps. cxxxii. 6).

10. Seir] not, of course, the mount of xi. 17.

Beth-shemesh] See xix. 22, 41 (Ir-shemesh), xxi. 16, 1 S.
vi. 9, 19. It is probably '*Ain es-Shems*, which lies on the main
high road between Joppa and Jerusalem, along which the railway
now runs. Permission has just been obtained for the excavation
of the site (*Pal. Expl. Fund: Quart. St.*, July 1910, pp. 174,
175, 220–231).

Timnah] a Philistine city, Jud. xiv. 1.

12 sea. And the west border was to the great sea, and the
border *thereof*. This is the border of the children of
Judah round about according to their families.

13-19. *The inheritance of Caleb.*

13 And unto Caleb the son of Jephunneh he gave a portion
among the children of Judah, according to the commandment of the LORD to Joshua, even Kiriath-arba, *which*
14 *Arba was* the father of Anak (the same is Hebron). And
Caleb drove out thence the three sons of Anak, Sheshai,
15 and Ahiman, and Talmai, the children of Anak. And he
went up thence against the inhabitants of Debir : now
16 the name of Debir beforetime was Kiriath-sepher. And
Caleb said, He that smiteth Kiriath-sepher, and taketh it,
17 to him will I give Achsah my daughter to wife. And
Othniel the son of Kenaz, the brother of Caleb, took it :
18 and he gave him Achsah his daughter to wife. And it
came to pass, when she came *unto him*, that she moved
him to ask of her father a field : and she lighted down

---

12. **And the west border** etc.] The reading should probably
be, **And the west border was the great sea for a border.** See
on xiii. 23, and cf. Numb. xxxiv. 6 (R.V. marg.).

13. This verse is editorial, serving as an introduction to the
account of Caleb's inheritance.

according to the commandment etc.] There is no record of
such a commandment to Joshua. See for the commandment to
Moses Num. xiv. 24, 30.

14-19. These verses are from an early source and are found
almost word for word in Jud. i. 10-15 Cf. on xi. 21.

14. **Sheshai** etc.] Cf. Num. xiii. 22.

15. **Debir** had been devoted by Joshua at the same time as
Hebron (x. 39). It was also called **Kiriath-sepher** and **Kiriath-
sannah** (*v.* 49), but no satisfactory meanings have been found for
these names.

17. **the son of Kenaz**] i.e. the Kenizzite (**son** = "descendant,"
as in vii. 24) ; see on xiv. 6.

18. **a field**] i.e., as the context implies, a well-watered tract
of land, most desirable in the Negeb (x. 40).

she lighted down] cf. Gen. xxiv. 64, 1 S. xxv. 23.
The original idea of the English verb is "to make light"
(sc. the burden of an animal by dismounting) ; hence the
meaning " to descend, come upon" (ii. 16).

from off her ass; and Caleb said unto her, What wouldest
thou? And she said, Give me a blessing; for that thou 19
hast set me in the land of the South, give me also springs
of water. And he gave her the upper springs and the
nether springs.

20-62. *The cities of Judah enumerated.*

The cities are placed (*a*) in the Negeb, *vv.* 21-32, (*b*) in the
Shephēlah, *vv.* 33-44, (*c*) in the hill country, *vv.* 48-60, and (*d*)
in the wilderness, *vv.* 61, 62. Some of the cities named in *vv.*
26-32, 42, belonged to Simeon (xix. 2-8).

This is the inheritance of the tribe of the children of 20
Judah according to their families.

And the uttermost cities of the tribe of the children of 21
Judah toward the border of Edom in the South were
Kabzeel, and Eder, and Jagur; and Kinah, and Dimonah, 22
and Adadah; and Kedesh, and Hazor, and Ithnan; Ziph, 23
and Telem, and Bealoth; and Hazor-hadattah, and 25
Kerioth-hezron (the same is Hazor); Amam, and Shema, 26
and Moladah; and Hazar-gaddah, and Heshmon, and 27
Beth-pelet; and Hazar-shual, and Beer-sheba, and Bizio- 28
thiah; Baalah, and Iim, and Ezem; and Eltolad, and 29
Chesil, and Hormah; and Ziklag, and Madmannah, and 31
Sansannah; and Lebaoth, and Shilhim, and Ain, and 32
Rimmon: all the cities are twenty and nine, with their
villages.

In the lowland, Eshtaol, and Zorah, and Ashnah; and 33
Zanoah, and En-gannim, Tappuah, and Enam; Jarmuth, 35
and Adullam, Socoh, and Azekah; and Shaaraim, and 36
Adithaim, and Gederah, and Gederothaim; fourteen
cities with their villages.

Zenan, and Hadashah, and Migdal-gad; and Dilan, 37,38

---

32. twenty and nine] The actual number is 36. Perhaps
an editor added names without altering the original total.
36. and Gederothaim] The Greek reads "and its farms,"
a correction which reduces the number to 14, in agreement with
the text.

39 and Mizpeh, and Joktheel; Lachish, and Bozkath, and
40 Eglon; and Cabbon, and Lahmam, and Chithlish; and
41 Gederoth, Beth-dagon, and Naamah, and Makkedah;
sixteen cities with their villages.

42
43   Libnah, and Ether, and Ashan; and Iphtah, and
44 Ashnab, and Nezib; and Keilah, and Achzib, and Mare-
·shah; nine cities with their villages.

45
46   Ekron, with her towns and her villages: from Ekron
even unto the sea, all that were by the side of Ashdod,
with their villages.

47   Ashdod, her towns and her villages; Gaza, her towns
and her villages; unto the brook of Egypt, and the great
sea, and the border *thereof*.

48   And in the hill country, Shamir, and Jattir, and Socoh;
49 and Dannah, and Kiriath-sannah (the same is Debir);
50
51 and Anab, and Eshtemoh, and Anim; and Goshen, and
Holon, and Giloh; eleven cities with their villages.

52
53   Arab, and Dumah, and Eshan; and Janim, and Beth-
54 tappuah, and Aphekah; and Humtah, and Kiriath-arba
(the same is Hebron), and Zior; nine cities with their
villages.

55
56   Maon, Carmel, and Ziph, and Jutah; and Jezreel, and
57 Jokdeam, and Zanoah; Kain, Gibeah, and Timnah; ten
cities with their villages.

58
59   Halhul, Beth-zur, and Gedor; and Maarath, and Beth-
anoth, and Eltekon; six cities with their villages.

60   Kiriath-baal (the same is Kiriath-jearim), and Rabbah;
two cities with their villages.

61   In the wilderness, Beth-arabah, Middin, and Secacah;
62 and Nibshan, and the City of Salt, and En-gedi; six
cities with their villages.

---

46. Ashdod] Read (LXX) **the slopes** (x. 40), the Heb. for
which might easily be confused with Ashdod (next verse).
62. the City of Salt perhaps lay in the valley of Salt (2 S.
viii. 13), at the southern end of the Salt Sea.

63. *A fragment concerning Jerusalem.*

And as for the Jebusites, the inhabitants of Jerusalem, 63 the children of Judah could not drive them out: but the Jebusites dwelt with the children of Judah at Jerusalem, unto this day.

xvi. 1–3. *The southern border of the children of Joseph.*

In this and the following chapter two accounts have been combined for the description of the inheritance of the children of Joseph. The first defines the southern border (xvi. 1–3), and then deals with the Manassites (xvii. 1, 2, 8, 11–13), but it only mentions the names of certain towns which ought to have been Manassite but were not. Imbedded in this there is a second, and later, account which deals with the Ephraimites (xvi. 5–9) and the Manassites (xvii. 7–10) separately. Two short stories are introduced: (*a*) the claim of the daughters of Zelophehad (xvii. 3–6), and (*b*) the request of the children of Joseph (xvii. 14–18). It is possible that the scantiness of the details relating to the inheritance of these important tribes, which is very apparent when a comparison is made with the full account of Judah's inheritance in ch. xv., is due to the fact that the land occupied by them formed part of the northern kingdom, and that when the Book of Joshua was assuming shape the northern kingdom had been swept away, and interest in the territory that once belonged to it had to a large extent ceased. Moreover, the hatred existing between the Samaritans (who occupied part of the territory in question) and the Jews would contribute to the silence of the post-exilic editors. See on ch. xix.

And the lot for the children of Joseph went out from 16 the Jordan at Jericho, at the waters of Jericho on the east, even the wilderness, going up from Jericho through the hill country to Beth-el; and it went out from Beth-el 2 to Luz, and passed along unto the border of the Archites

---

63. This verse = Jud. i. 21 (where, however, Benjamin, not Judah, is the subject). There was evidently a tradition that Jerusalem belonged to Benjamin (see *v.* 8, xviii. 28), but the present verse makes it Judaean.

xvi. 1–3. Cf. the northern border of Benjamin in xviii. 12–14.

1. **at the waters of Jericho**] A gloss on **Jericho**.

2. **Beth-el...Luz**] Apparently the same place (xviii. 13, Gen. xxxv. 6, Jud. i. 23); hence **to Luz** must be a gloss.

the Archites] In 2 S. xv. 32 Hushai the Archite is mentioned,

3 to Ataroth ; and it went down westward to the border of the Japhletites, unto the border of Beth-horon the nether, even unto Gezer : and the goings out thereof were at the sea.

4-9.   The border of Ephraim.

4 And the children of Joseph, Manasseh and Ephraim, took 5 their inheritance.   And the border of the children of Ephraim according to their families was *thus* : even the border of their inheritance eastward was Ataroth-addar, 6 unto Beth-horon the upper ; and the border went out westward at Michmethath on the north ; and the border turned about eastward unto Taanath-shiloh, and passed 7 along it on the east of Janoah ; and it went down from Janoah to Ataroth, and to Naarah, and reached unto 8 Jericho, and went out at Jordan.   From Tappuah the border went along westward to the brook of Kanah ; and the goings out thereof were at the sea.   This is the inheritance of the tribe of the children of Ephraim ac- 9 cording to their families ; together with the cities which were separated for the children of Ephraim in the midst of the inheritance of the children of Manasseh, all the cities with their villages.

10.   A fragment concerning Gezer (cf. Jud. i. 29).

10 And they drave not out the Canaanites that dwelt in Gezer : but the Canaanites dwelt in the midst of Ephraim, unto this day, and became servants to do taskwork.

---

but nothing is known of the people.   **Atâroth**, if correct, is a different place from that mentioned in *v.* 7, but it appears to be a gloss.

3.   The **Japhlĕtites** are unknown.

4.   Manasseh and Ephraim] So xiv. 4, xvii. 1.   On the precedence given to Ephraim see the story in Gen. xlviii. 8–20. The editor has followed this in placing the description of the Ephraimite inheritance before that of Manasseh (cf. xvii. 17).

6–8.   Cf. xvii. 7–9.

9.   together with] Heb. **and.**   The verse had no connexion originally with the preceding section.

And *this* was the lot for the tribe of Manasseh ; for he **17** was the firstborn of Joseph.   As for Machir the firstborn of Manasseh, the father of Gilead, because he was a man of war, therefore he had Gilead and Bashan.   And *the* **2** *lot* was for the rest of the children of Manasseh according to their families ; for the children of Abiezer, and for the children of Helek, and for the children of Asriel, and for the children of Shechem, and for the children of Hepher, and for the children of Shemida : these were the male children of Manasseh the son of Joseph according to their families.

But Zelophehad, the son of Hepher, the son of Gilead, **3** the son of Machir, the son of Manasseh, had no sons, but daughters : and these are the names of his daughters, Mahlah, and Noah, Hoglah, Milcah, and Tirzah.   And **4** they came near before Eleazar the priest, and before Joshua the son of Nun, and before the princes, saying, The LORD commanded Moses to give us an inheritance among our brethren : therefore according to the commandment of the LORD he gave them an inheritance among the brethren of their father.

And there fell ten parts to Manasseh, beside the land of **5** Gilead and Bashan, which is beyond Jordan ; because **6** the daughters of Manasseh had an inheritance among his sons : and the land of Gilead belonged unto the rest of

---

xvii. 1.   **Machir**, an old name for Manasseh (Jud. v. 14), is called **the father of Gilead** as having taken Gilead in possession (see on xiii. 29).

5.   **the land of Gilead.**   See on xii. 2.

7 the sons of Manasseh. And the border of Manasseh was
from Asher to Michmethath, which is before Shechem ;
and the border went along to the right hand, unto the
8 inhabitants of En-tappuah. The land of Tappuah belonged to Manasseh : but Tappuah on the border of
9 Manasseh belonged to the children of Ephraim. And
the border went down unto the brook of Kanah, southward of the brook : these cities belonged to Ephraim
among the cities of Manasseh : and the border of Manasseh was on the north side of the brook, and the goings
10 out thereof were at the sea : southward it was Ephraim's,
and northward it was Manasseh's, and the sea was his
border ; and they reached to Asher on the north, and to
11 Issachar on the east. And Manasseh had in Issachar
and in Asher Beth-shean and her towns, and Ibleam and
her towns, and the inhabitants of Dor and her towns, and
the inhabitants of En-dor and her towns, and the inhabitants of Taanach and her towns, and the inhabitants of

---

7–9. Cf. xvi. 6–8.

7. Shechem] See on xx. 7.

to the right hand] i.e. to the south.

9. these cities etc.] a fragment from another document.

10. they reached] The subject must be *the children of
Joseph* (xvi. 4).

11–13. An extract from an older source. See Jud. i. 27, 28.

11. Beth-shean (the later Scythopolis, a few miles from the
Jordan), **Ibleam** (S. of Jezreel), **Dor** (xi. 2), **Taanach** and **Megiddo**
(mentioned together in xii. 21, Jud. v. 19), were all important
places commanding the plain of Jezreel (*v.* 16, or Megiddo, or
Esdraelon). The Canaanites, so long as they retained possession of these towns, not only enjoyed a rich and fertile tract of
country (cf. Hos. ii. 22), but also were enabled to cut off com-
munication between the north and south of the land. Hence
the stubborn resistance mentioned in the text. **En-dor** is not
mentioned in *Judges* and is probably a mistake, which crept
into the text from a confusion with Dor. It lies just south of
Mt. Tabor and is therefore too far north to be intended here.
On **Taanach** and **Megiddo**, and the results of recent excavations
there, see Driver, *Modern Research*, pp. 10, 33, 80–85.

Megiddo and her towns, even the three heights.　Yet the 12
children of Manasseh could not drive out *the inhabitants
of* those cities ; but the Canaanites would dwell in that
land.　And it came to pass, when the children of Israel 13
were waxen strong, that they put the Canaanites to taskwork, and did not utterly drive them out.

14–18. *The request of the children of Joseph.*

This section seems to be an extract from an old story which
described the departure of some Manassites to Gilead (cf. on xiii.
29).　Notice the vague description of the district intended and
the suppression of the conclusion.

And the children of Joseph spake unto Joshua, saying, 14
Why hast thou given me but one lot and one part for
an inheritance, seeing I am a great people, forasmuch as
hitherto the LORD hath blessed me?　And Joshua said 15
unto them, If thou be a great people, get thee up to the
forest, and cut down for thyself there in the land of the
Perizzites and of the Rephaim ; since the hill country of
Ephraim is too narrow for thee.　And the children of 16
Joseph said, The hill country is not enough for us : and
all the Canaanites that dwell in the land of the valley
have chariots of iron, both they who are in Beth-shean
and her towns, and they who are in the valley of Jezreel.

---

the three heights]　The marg. refers to xi. 2 and xii. 23: but the
Heb. text is probably corrupt.　LXX reads the name of a place.

13.　waxen]　*To wax* is A.-S., allied to the German *wachsen*
(= "to grow ").　Cf. Gen. xviii. 12, xix. 13, etc.

15.　the forest]　Perhaps that mentioned in 2 Sam. xviii. 6,
of which however nothing is known.

the land of the Perizzites and of the Rephaim]　The Perizzites are here named with the Rephaim (xii. 4), whose land (Dt.
iii. 13) was Bashan, on the east of Jordan.　They also appear in
the list of peoples to be dispossessed by Israel (e.g. iii. 10).　But
nothing is known of them.

the hill country of Ephraim]　The chief feature of the
Ephraimite territory gives its name to the whole.

16.　chariots of iron]　See on vi. 19, xi. 4.

Jezreel]　See on xix. 18.

17 And Joshua spake unto the house of Joseph, even to
Ephraim and to Manasseh, saying, Thou art a great
people, and hast great power : thou shalt not have one
18 lot only : but the hill country shall be thine ; for though
it is a forest, thou shalt cut it down, and the goings out
thereof shall be thine : for thou shalt drive out the Canaanites, though they have chariots of iron, and though
they be strong.

xviii. 1-10. *Arrangements for the division of the land amongst
the seven tribes which had not as yet received their inheritance.*

On the opening verses of this chapter see on xiii. 1.
Chs. xviii. 11–xix. 51 contain the late Priestly account of the
division of the remainder of the land amongst the seven tribes.
It was originally prefaced by xviii. 1 (as a general introduction)
and also by portions of xiv.–xvii. (dealing with the settlement of
Judah, Manasseh, and Ephraim). Thus a fairly consecutive
narrative of the allotment of Western Canaan can be restored. It
represents that allotment as taking place at one assembly of the
people at Shiloh, under the direction of " Eleazar the priest and
Joshua the son of Nun " (xiv. 1, xviii. 1, xix. 51).

xviii. 2-10 form a section from an earlier document, which
offers a marked contrast to the other account in making Joshua
the sole agent in the allotment (*vv.* 3, 10). It has passed through
the hands of an editor, to whom we owe the explanatory note in
v. 7, and also the insertion of **Shiloh** (*vv.* 8-10), made to
harmonize with *v.* 1.

18　　　And the whole congregation of the children of Israel
assembled themselves together at Shiloh, and set up the
tent of meeting there : and the land was subdued before
2 them.　　And there remained among the children of Israel

---

18. the hill country] i.e. of Gilead (Num. xxxii. 39).

xviii. 1. Shiloh] About 12 miles N. of Jerusalem and the
seat of the Ark in the days of Samuel (1 S. i.–iv.). After the
conquest it took, according to this verse, the place of Gilgal as
the religious centre of the nation. C1. 1 S. i. 3, Ps. lxxviii. 60.

the tent of meeting] i.e. the tent where Jehovah met with his
people (Ex. xxv. 22, xxxiii. 7, Num. xvii. 4). See further on
xxii. 19.

and the land etc.] Rather, **for the land had been subdued.**

seven tribes, which had not yet divided their inheritance. And Joshua said unto the children of Israel, How long 3 are ye slack to go in to possess the land, which the LORD, the God of your fathers, hath given you? Appoint for 4 you three men for each tribe: and I will send them, and they shall arise, and walk through the land, and describe it according to their inheritance; and they shall come unto me. And they shall divide it into seven portions: 5 Judah shall abide in his border on the south, and the house of Joseph shall abide in their border on the north. And ye shall describe the land into seven portions, and 6 bring *the description* hither to me: and I will cast lots for you here before the LORD our God. For the Levites 7 have no portion among you; for the priesthood of the LORD is their inheritance: and Gad and Reuben and the half tribe of Manasseh have received their inheritance beyond Jordan eastward, which Moses the servant of the LORD gave them. And the men arose, and went: and 8 Joshua charged them that went to describe the land, saying, Go and walk through the land, and describe it, and come again to me, and I will cast lots for you here before the LORD in Shiloh. And the men went and 9 passed through the land, and described it by cities into seven portions in a book, and they came to Joshua unto the camp at Shiloh. And Joshua cast lots for them 10 in Shiloh before the LORD: and there Joshua divided the land unto the children of Israel according to their divisions.

---

4. **describe**] Lit. **write** (so Jud. viii. 14).
according to their inheritance] Apparently the commissioners were to arrange the inheritances amongst themselves; but this is contrary to *vv.* 6, 10.
7. **the priesthood of the LORD**] See Dt. x. 8.
10. **for them**] i.e. for the seven tribes.

11-28. *The inheritance of Benjamin.*

11　And the lot of the tribe of the children of Benjamin
came up according to their families : and the border of
their lot went out between the children of Judah and
12 the children of Joseph. And their border on the north
quarter was from Jordan ; and the border went up to the
side of Jericho on the north, and went up through the
hill country westward ; and the goings out thereof were
13 at the wilderness of Beth-aven. And the border passed
along from thence to Luz, to the side of Luz (the same
is Beth-el), southward ; and the border went down to
Ataroth-addar, by the mountain that lieth on the south
14 of Beth-horon the nether. And the border was drawn
and turned about on the west quarter southward, from
the mountain that lieth before Beth-horon southward ;
and the goings out thereof were at Kiriath-baal (the same
is Kiriath-jearim), a city of the children of Judah : this
15 was the west quarter. And the south quarter was from
the uttermost part of Kiriath-jearim, and the border
went out westward, and went out to the fountain of the
16 waters of Nephtoah : and the border went down to the
uttermost part of the mountain that lieth before the valley
of the son of Hinnom, which is in the vale of Rephaim
northward ; and it went down to the valley of Hinnom,
to the side of the Jebusite southward, and went down to
17 En-rogel ; and it was drawn on the north, and went out
at En-shemesh, and went out to Geliloth, which is over
against the ascent of Adummim ; and it went down to
18 the stone of Bohan the son of Reuben ; and it passed
along to the side over against the Arabah northward, and
19 went down unto the Arabah : and the border passed

14.　**Kiriath-jearim**]　See on xv. 9.
18.　**the Arabah**] perhaps shortened from Beth-arābah (*v.* 22,
xv. 6, 61).

along to the side of Beth-hoglah northward : and the
goings out of the border were at the north bay of the
Salt Sea, at the south end of Jordan : this was the south
border.   And Jordan was the border of it on the east 20
quarter.   This was the inheritance of the children of
Benjamin, by the borders thereof round about, according
to their families.   Now the cities of the tribe of the 21
children of Benjamin according to their families were
Jericho, and Beth-hoglah, and Emek-keziz ; and Beth- 22
arabah, and Zemaraim, and Beth-el ; and Avvim, and 23
Parah, and Ophrah ; and Chephar-ammoni, and Ophni, 24
and Geba ; twelve cities with their villages : Gibeon, and 25
Ramah, and Beeroth ; and Mizpeh, and Chephirah, and 26
Mozah ; and Rekem, and Irpeel, and Taralah ; and $^{27}_{28}$
Zelah, Eleph, and the Jebusite (the same is Jerusalem),
Gibeath, *and* Kiriath ; fourteen cities with their villages.
This is the inheritance of the children of Benjamin
according to their families.

xix. 1-9. *The inheritance of Simeon.*

The plan of the Priestly writer in dealing with the settlement
of the tribes was to give an outline of the border and then to
enumerate the cities belonging to each.   The editors have in
a fairly complete manner preserved this writer's accounts of the
inheritances of Judah (xv.) and Benjamin (xviii.), inasmuch as
members of these two tribes formed the bulk of the returned
exiles, and interest in their possessions naturally ran high ; but
with Manasseh and Ephraim they dealt very severely (see on ch.
xvi.).   The original descriptions of the remaining six tribes, with
which the present chapter is concerned, have also suffered to a
great extent, and the borders and the cities which have been
allowed to remain in the text, are neither complete nor free from
confusion.

---

23. Ophrah] not the place with which Gideon was connected
(Jud. vi. 11–24).

25–28. Gibeon ... Beeroth ... Chephirah ... Kiriath] ix. 17.
Kiriath is a part of the name Kiriath-jearim.

28. Gibeath, i.e. Gibeah.   There were probably two places
so called in Benjamin, Gibeah of Saul (1 S. xi. 4), and Gibeah of
Benjamin (1 S. xiii. 2).

19 And the second lot came out for Simeon, even for the tribe of the children of Simeon according to their families: and their inheritance was in the midst of the inheritance
2 of the children of Judah. And they had for their inherit-
3 ance Beer-sheba, or Sheba, and Moladah; and Hazar-
4 shual, and Balah, and Ezem; and Eltolad, and Bethul,
5 and Hormah; and Ziklag, and Beth-marcaboth, and
6 Hazar-susah; and Beth-lebaoth, and Sharuhen; thirteen
7 cities with their villages: Ain, Rimmon, and Ether, and
8 Ashan; four cities with their villages: and all the villages that were round about these cities to Baalath-beer, Ramah of the South. This is the inheritance of the tribe of the children of Simeon according to their families.
9 Out of the part of the children of Judah was the inherit- ance of the children of Simeon: for the portion of the children of Judah was too much for them: therefore the children of Simeon had inheritance in the midst of their inheritance.

10–16. *The inheritance of Zebulun.*

10 And the third lot came up for the children of Zebulun according to their families: and the border of their in-
11 heritance was unto Sarid: and their border went up westward, even to Maralah, and reached to Dabbesheth;
12 and it reached to the brook that is before Jokneam; and it turned from Sarid eastward toward the sunrising unto the border of Chisloth-tabor; and it went out to Daberath,
13 and went up to Japhia; and from thence it passed along eastward to Gath-hepher, to Eth-kazin; and it went out

---

xix. 1. and their inheritance etc.] Cf. *v.* 9. The absence of any notice about a Simeonite *border* is thus explained.

2. or Sheba] Heb. **and Sheba**, which being a scribe's repeti- tion of the previous name would make the total of *v.* 6 correct.

10. Sarid] represents the most southerly point of Zebulun's territory. In *v.* 11 the southern border is traced *westward*, and in *v.* 12 *eastward*, from this place.

at Rimmon which stretcheth unto Neah; and the border 14
turned about it on the north to Hannathon: and the
goings out thereof were at the valley of Iphtah-el; and 15
Kattath, and Nahalal, and Shimron, and Idalah, and
Beth-lehem: twelve cities with their villages. This is 16
the inheritance of the children of Zebulun according to
their families, these cities with their villages.

17–23.　*The inheritance of Issachar.*

The fourth lot came out for Issachar, even for the 17
children of Issachar according to their families. And 18
their border was unto Jezreel, and Chesulloth, and
Shunem; and Hapharaim, and Shion, and Anaharath; 19
and Rabbith, and Kishion, and Ebez; and Remeth, and 20 21
En-gannim, and En-haddah, and Beth-pazzez; and the 22
border reached to Tabor, and Shahazumah, and Beth-
shemesh; and the goings out of their border were at
Jordan: sixteen cities with their villages. This is the 23
inheritance of the tribe of the children of Issachar according to their families, the cities with their villages.

24–31.　*The inheritance of Asher.*

Here, again, there is confusion between the borders and the
cities.

And the fifth lot came out for the tribe of the children 24

---

15. These five cities are a fragment of the complete list
which contained twelve names. Not only have the names of
cities dropped out, but also a portion of the description of the
border, viz. the western.

Beth-lehem] Six miles N.W. of Nazareth.

18. Read:—**And their border was unto—**. The names defining
the *border* have been lost. The list of *cities* begins with **Jezreel,
and Chesulloth.**

Jezreel] From this important place the Plain of Jezreel
derived its name (see on xvii. 11). Its actual site has not yet
been discovered, though it is believed by many to be *Zer'in*.

22.　sixteen cities] i.e. inclusive of the three just mentioned
and which belong to the delineation of the border.

25 of Asher according to their families. And their border
26 was Helkath, and Hali, and Beten, and Achshaph ; and
Allammelech, and Amad, and Mishal ; and it reached to
27 Carmel westward, and to Shihor-libnath ; and it turned
toward the sunrising to Beth-dagon, and reached to
Zebulun, and to the valley of Iphtah-el northward to
Beth-emek and Neiel ; and it went out to Cabul on the
28 left hand, and Ebron, and Rehob, and Hammon, and
29 Kanah, even unto great Zidon ; and the border turned to
Ramah, and to the fenced city of Tyre ; and the border
turned to Hosah ; and the goings out thereof were at the
30 sea by the region of Achzib : Ummah also, and Aphek,
and Rehob : twenty and two cities with their villages.
31 This is the inheritance of the tribe of the children of
Asher according to their families, these cities with their
villages.

32-39. *The inheritance of Naphtali.*

32   The sixth lot came out for the children of Naphtali,
even for the children of Naphtali according to their
33 families. And their border was from Heleph, from the
oak in Zaanannim, and Adami-nekeb, and Jabneel, unto
Lakkum ; and the goings out thereof were at Jordan :
34 and the border turned westward to Aznoth-tabor, and
went out from thence to Hukkok ; and it reached to
Zebulun on the south, and reached to Asher on the west,

---

25. Read :—**And their border was**—The continuation is lost,
as in *v.* 18.

27. **on the left hand**] i.e. on the north (cf. xvii. 7).

28. **Rehob**] repeated in *v.* 30.

29. **by the region of Achzib**] marg. "Or, *from Hebel· to
Achzib.*" But it is better to adopt a slight change in the Heb.
text and to read **Mahalab** [and] **Achzib**, Mahalab being the
Ahlab of Jud. i. 31.

30. **twenty and two**] There are 24 actually named, and if
either of the suggestions mentioned in *v.* 29 be adopted the
total will be 25. See on xv. 32.

and to Judah at Jordan toward the sunrising. And the 35
fenced cities were Ziddim, Zer, and Hammath, Rakkath,
and Chinnereth ; and Adamah, and Ramah, and Hazor; 36
and Kedesh, and Edrei, and En-hazor; and Iron, and $^{37}_{38}$
Migdal-el, Horem, and Beth-anath, and Beth-shemesh ;
nineteen cities with their villages. This is the inheritance 39
of the tribe of the children of Naphtali according to their
families, the cities with their villages.

40–48.   *The inheritance of Dan.*

No attempt at a delineation of border is made. Dan could
hardly have aspired to one, seeing that its inheritance lay almost
entirely in the territory of the Philistines, and as the result shows
it was unable to retain it.

The seventh lot came out for the tribe of the children 40
of Dan according to their families. And the border of 41
their inheritance was Zorah, and Eshtaol, and Ir-shemesh ;
and Shaalabbin, and Aijalon, and Ithlah ; and Elon, and $^{42}_{43}$
Timnah, and Ekron ; and Eltekeh, and Gibbethon, and 44
Baalath ; and Jehud, and Bene-berak, and Gath-rimmon; 45
and Me-jarkon, and Rakkon, with the border over against 46
Joppa. And the border of the children of Dan went out 47
beyond them : for the children of Dan went up and
fought against Leshem, and took it, and smote it with

---

34. to Judah] Evidently a mistake. Perhaps the original
text had *Jahŭlah*, a place about 2 miles N. of Lake Ḥuleh.
  37. Kedesh] N.W. of Lake Ḥuleh. See xii. 22, xx. 7,
Jud. iv. 6.
  38. nineteen] As in *vv*. 35–38 only sixteen appear, three
names must have been lost.
  47. And the border...beyond them] i.e. the border was lost
to them (cf. Lam. i. 6). The words are an editorial introduction to the quotation that follows.
  for the children of Dan...their father] A quotation from
an earlier document. The reason of this migration of Dan is
given in Jud. i. 34–36, and the story of it in Jud. xviii.
  Leshem] i.e. Laish (Jud. xviii. 7 etc.), situated in the extreme
north of the land. To mark the success of the migration the place

the edge of the sword, and possessed it, and dwelt therein, and called Leshem, Dan, after the name of Dan their 48 father. This is the inheritance of the tribe of the children of Dan according to their families, these cities with their villages.

49-51. *Concluding notices of the allotment of the land, and the inheritance of Joshua.*

49 So they made an end of distributing the land for inheritance by the borders thereof; and the children of Israel gave an inheritance to Joshua the son of Nun in 50 the midst of them: according to the commandment of the LORD they gave him the city which he asked, even Timnath-serah in the hill country of Ephraim: and he built the city, and dwelt therein.

51 These are the inheritances, which Eleazar the priest, and Joshua the son of Nun, and the heads of the fathers' *houses* of the tribes of the children of Israel, distributed for inheritance by lot in Shiloh before the LORD, at the door of the tent of meeting. So they made an end of dividing the land.

xx. 1-9. *The appointment of the Cities of Refuge.*

In the laws of Israel murder was forbidden (Ex. xxi. 12, Lev. xxiv. 17); but if it was committed it became the duty of the next of kin (who was called "the avenger of blood," *v.* 3, 2 S. xiv. 11) to compass the death of the murderer, a duty which was ruthlessly carried out (Jud. viii. 18-21, 2 S. iii. 27). This terrible custom, which was general amongst Semitic peoples, naturally led to many evils, not the least of which was that it might involve

---

was re-named Dan, and as such often appears in the expression "from Dan to Beer-sheba" (2 S. xvii. 11).

49, 50. An extract from an earlier document.

49. they] i.e. apparently **the children of Israel.**

50. according to the commandment etc.] There is no record of this.

Timnath-serah] xxiv. 30, Jud. ii. 9. It lay about 14 miles eastward from Joppa.

the death of the innocent. Hence grew up the right of asylum, the asylum being originally any sanctuary where "the manslayer that killeth any person unwittingly" might take protection (Ex. xxi. 13, 14, 1 K. i. 50). It must have been extremely rare for this right to be abused (1 K. ii. 28–34). As the Law of Deuteronomy recognised only one sanctuary and one altar, namely at Jerusalem, it became necessary to make some new arrangement. Thus certain cities were set aside (Dt. iv. 41–43, xix. 1–10), which in the late Priestly work, upon which the present chapter is based (cf. Num. xxxv. 9–15), received the name of "Cities of Refuge."

And the LORD spake unto Joshua, saying, Speak to **20** the children of Israel, saying, Assign you the cities of 2 refuge, whereof I spake unto you by the hand of Moses: that the manslayer that killeth any person unwittingly 3 *and* unawares may flee thither: and they shall be unto you for a refuge from the avenger of blood. And he 4 shall flee unto one of those cities, and shall stand at the entering of the gate of the city, and declare his cause in the ears of the elders of that city; and they shall take him into the city unto them, and give him a place, that he may dwell among them. And if the avenger of blood 5 pursue after him, then they shall not deliver up the manslayer into his hand; because he smote his neighbour unawares, and hated him not beforetime. And he shall 6 dwell in that city, until he stand before the congregation for judgement, until the death of the high priest that shall be in those days: then shall the manslayer return, and come unto his own city, and unto his own house, unto

---

xx. 3. unwittingly] undesignedly (marg. *through error*). The word **unawares** is an insertion; cf. Dt. iv. 42.

4. at the entering of the gate] where meetings were held and justice administered. Cf. Dt. xxi. 19, Ruth iv. 1, 2, 2 S. xv. 2.

6. until he stand…until the death…] Two divergent timelimits, the result of the combination of two accounts. The LXX bears witness to a simpler account, as it omits *vv.* 4–6 with the exception of the words **until he stand before the congregation for judgement.**

7 the city from whence he fled. And they set apart Kedesh in Galilee in the hill country of Naphtali, and Shechem in the hill country of Ephraim, and Kiriath-arba (the same 8 is Hebron) in the hill country of Judah. And beyond the Jordan at Jericho eastward, they assigned Bezer in the wilderness in the plain out of the tribe of Reuben, and Ramoth in Gilead out of the tribe of Gad, and Golan in 9 Bashan out of the tribe of Manasseh. These were the appointed cities for all the children of Israel, and for the stranger that sojourneth among them, that whosoever killeth any person unwittingly might flee thither, and not die by the hand of the avenger of blood, until he stood before the congregation.

xxi. 1–3. *The Levites ask for their promised inheritance and obtain it.*

By the provisions of the older Law (xiii. 14, 33, xiv. 3, xviii. 7, Numb. xviii. 20, Dt. x. 9, xviii. 1, 2) "the priests the Levites" had no inheritance as the other tribes, but they were maintained by certain privileges and bounties (cf. Dt. xii. 11, 12, 19, xxvi. 12, 1 S. ii. 12–17). According to the late Priestly writer, however (cf. xiv. 4, Num. xxxv. 1–8, 1 Chr. vi. 54–81), forty-eight cities were assigned to them by a divine command given to Moses. The fulfilment of this command is recorded in the present chapter, but a distinction is made in assigning 13 cities to the Priests (*v.* 19) and 35 to the Levites (*vv.* 26, 33, 40).

That this ordinance is an ideal one is evident, not only from its contradiction to the older Law, but also from the fact that (1) some of the cities named were non-Levitical (e.g. Hebron,

---

7. set apart] marg. "Heb. *sanctified.*"

Shechem] An important town and sanctuary, occupying a central position in the land (see on viii. 30–35). Cf. xvii. 7, xxiv. 1, 32, Gen. xxxiii. 18–20.

8. at Jericho] is meaningless. A scribe has repeated it mechanically from some such passage as xiii. 32. The LXX omits it.

Bezer] The southernmost city, but the site is unknown.

Ramoth in Gilead] 1 K. iv. 13, xxii. 3; perhaps *er-Remthe*, six miles S.W. of *Der'ât*.

Golan] Perhaps *saḥem el-Golan*, about 15 miles E. of the Sea of Galilee.

xiv. 13 ; Shechem, Jud. ix. ; Jattir and Eshtemoa, 1 S. xxx. 27, 28) : (2) the priests dwelt in cities which do not occur in this list (Nob, 1 S. xxii. 19, Shiloh, 1 S. i. 3, 4) : (3) some of the cities (Gezer, Taanach) were not in the possession of Israel in the days of Joshua : and (4) the distinction between Priests and Levites is post-exilic (cf. on iii. 3).

Then came near the heads of fathers' *houses* of the **21** Levites unto Eleazar the priest, and unto Joshua the son of Nun, and unto the heads of fathers' *houses* of the tribes of the children of Israel ; and they spake unto them at 2 Shiloh in the land of Canaan, saying, The LORD commanded by the hand of Moses to give us cities to dwell in, with the suburbs thereof for our cattle. And the 3 children of Israel gave unto the Levites out of their inheritance, according to the commandment of the LORD, these cities with their suburbs.

4–7. *The number of cities allotted.*

And the lot came out for the families of the Kohathites: 4 and the children of Aaron the priest, which were of the Levites, had by lot out of the tribe of Judah, and out of the tribe of the Simeonites, and out of the tribe of Benjamin, thirteen cities.

And the rest of the children of Kohath had by lot out 5 of the families of the tribe of Ephraim, and out of the tribe of Dan, and out of the half tribe of Manasseh, ten cities.

And the children of Gershon had by lot out of the 6 families of the tribe of Issachar, and out of the tribe of Asher, and out of the tribe of Naphtali, and out of the half tribe of Manasseh in Bashan, thirteen cities.

The children of Merari according to their families had 7

---

xxi. 2. suburbs] pasture lands, as xiv. 4.
4. According to Ex. vi. 16 Gershon, Kohath, and Merari were the sons of Levi. The Kohathites take the precedence here, as Aaron belonged to this branch (Ex. vi. 18, 20).

out of the tribe of Reuben, and out of the tribe of Gad, and out of the tribe of Zebulun, twelve cities.

8–12. *Introductory notice to the list containing the names of the cities.*

8 And the children of Israel gave by lot unto the Levites these cities with their suburbs, as the LORD commanded
9 by the hand of Moses. And they gave out of the tribe of the children of Judah, and out of the tribe of the children of Simeon, these cities which are *here* mentioned
10 by name : and they were for the children of Aaron, of the families of the Kohathites, who were of the children of
11 Levi : for theirs was the first lot. And they gave them Kiriath-arba, *which Arba was* the father of Anak, (the same is Hebron,) in the hill country of Judah, with the
12 suburbs thereof round about it. But the fields of the city, and the villages thereof, gave they to Caleb the son of Jephunneh for his possession.

13–19. *Names of the Priestly cities.*

13 And unto the children of Aaron the priest they gave Hebron with her suburbs, the city of refuge for the man-
14 slayer, and Libnah with her suburbs ; and Jattir with her
15 suburbs, and Eshtemoa with her suburbs ; and Holon
16 with her suburbs, and Debir with her suburbs ; and Ain with her suburbs, and Juttah with her suburbs, *and* Beth-shemesh with her suburbs ; nine cities out of those two
17 tribes. And out of the tribe of Benjamin, Gibeon with
18 her suburbs, Geba with her suburbs ; Anathoth with her
19 suburbs, and Almon with her suburbs ; four cities. All

11, 12 must be read as a parenthesis. They have been inserted for the purpose of explaining how Hebron could be said to belong to Caleb (xiv. 6–15) and yet be an Aaronic city.

12.   **But the fields** etc.]   Rather, **Now the fields...they had given**...

16.   **those two tribes**] i.e. Judah and Simeon (*v.* 9).

the cities of the children of Aaron, the priests, were thirteen cities with their suburbs.

20–40. *Names of the Levitical cities.*

And the families of the children of Kohath, the Levites, 20 even the rest of the children of Kohath, they had the cities of their lot out of the tribe of Ephraim.   And they gave 21 them Shechem with her suburbs in the hill country of Ephraim, the city of refuge for the manslayer, and Gezer with her suburbs ; and Kibzaim with her suburbs, and 22 Beth-horon with her suburbs ; four cities.   And out of 23 the tribe of Dan, Elteke with her suburbs, Gibbethon with her suburbs ; Aijalon with her suburbs, Gath-rimmon 24 with her suburbs ; four cities.   And out of the half tribe 25 of Manasseh, Taanach with her suburbs, and Gath-rim-mon with her suburbs ; two cities.   All the cities of the 26 families of the rest of the children of Kohath were ten with their suburbs.

And unto the children of Gershon, of the families of 27 the Levites, out of the half tribe of Manasseh *they gave* Golan in Bashan with her suburbs, the city of refuge for the manslayer ; and Be-eshterah with her suburbs ; two cities.   And out of the tribe of Issachar, Kishion with 28 her suburbs, Daberath with her suburbs ; Jarmuth with 29 her suburbs, En-gannim with her suburbs ; four cities. And out of the tribe of Asher, Mishal with her suburbs, 30 Abdon with her suburbs ; Helkath with her suburbs, and 31 Rehob with her suburbs ; four cities.   And out of the 32 tribe of Naphtali, Kedesh in Galilee with her suburbs, the city of refuge for the manslayer, and Hammoth-dor with her suburbs, and Kartan with her suburbs ; three cities. All the cities of the Gershonites according to their families 33 were thirteen cities with their suburbs.

And unto the families of the children of Merari, the 34 rest of the Levites, out of the tribe of Zebulun, Jokneam

35 with her suburbs, and Kartah with her suburbs, Dimnah
with her suburbs, Nahalal with her suburbs ; four cities.
36 And out of the tribe of Reuben, Bezer with her suburbs,
37 and Jahaz with her suburbs, Kedemoth with her suburbs,
38 and Mephaath with her suburbs ; four cities. And out
of the tribe of Gad, Ramoth in Gilead with her suburbs,
the city of refuge for the manslayer, and Mahanaim with
39 her suburbs ; Heshbon with her suburbs, Jazer with her
40 suburbs ; four cities in all. All *these were* the cities of
the children of Merari according to their families, even
the rest of the families of the Levites ; and their lot was
twelve cities.

41, 42. *Concluding notice.*

41   All the cities of the Levites in the midst of the possession
of the children of Israel were forty and eight cities with
42 their suburbs. These cities were every one with their
suburbs round about them : thus it was with all these
cities.

43-45. *Notice by the editor, summing up the general results of the conquest.*

This notice would have been more suitable at the close of
ch. xii.

43   So the LORD gave unto Israel all the land which he
sware to give unto their fathers ; and they possessed it,
44 and dwelt therein. And the LORD gave them rest round
about, according to all that he sware unto their fathers :
and there stood not a man of all their enemies before
them ; the LORD delivered all their enemies into their
45 hand. There failed not aught of any good thing which
the LORD had spoken unto the house of Israel ; all came
to pass.

---

44. there stood not a man etc.]   See on i. 5.
45. of any good thing]   Rather, **of all the good things.**

PART III. CHAPTERS XXII–XXIV.

APPENDICES, DEALING WITH THE CLOSE OF JOSHUA'S WORK.

xxii. 1–8. *Joshua blesses the trans-Jordanic tribes and sends them away.*

Then Joshua called the Reubenites, and the Gadites, 22 and the half tribe of Manasseh, and said unto them, Ye 2 have kept all that Moses the servant of the LORD commanded you, and have hearkened unto my voice in all that I commanded you: ye have not left your brethren 3 these many days unto this day, but have kept the charge of the commandment of the LORD your God. And now 4 the LORD your God hath given rest unto your brethren, as he spake unto them: therefore now turn ye, and get you unto your tents, unto the land of your possession, which Moses the servant of the LORD gave you beyond Jordan. Only take diligent heed to do the commandment 5 and the law, which Moses the servant of the LORD commanded you, to love the LORD your God, and to walk in all his ways, and to keep his commandments, and to cleave unto him, and to serve him with all your heart and with all your soul. So Joshua blessed them, and 6 sent them away: and they went unto their tents.

Now to the one half tribe of Manasseh Moses had 7 given *inheritance* in Bashan: but unto the other half gave Joshua among their brethren beyond Jordan westward. Moreover when Joshua sent them away unto their tents, he blessed them, and spake unto them, saying, 8

---

xxii. 4. tents] So *vv.* 6–8. As the Israelites after the conquest lived in the cities they had taken, the word **tents** here must be a reminiscence of their earlier life, and one indeed which survived till later times (contrast 1 S. viii. 22 with 1 S. iv. 10).

7, 8. A fragment from another source. Eastern Manasseh has already gone away (*v.* 6).

8. For the division of the spoil cf. Num. xxxi. 25–27, 1 S. xxx. 24, 2 Macc. viii. 28, 30.

Return with much wealth unto your tents, and with very much cattle, with silver, and with gold, and with brass, and with iron, and with very much raiment: divide the spoil of your enemies with your brethren.

> *9-12. The erection of an altar by the trans-Jordanic tribes, and the indignation of their brethren.*

The incident as recorded here (*vv.* 9-34) cannot be historical. It assumes that the altar was illegal because it was "besides [in addition to] the altar of the LORD our God" (*vv.* 19, 29), that is, the official altar at Shiloh (xviii. 1). The idea underlying the story is, therefore, that one altar alone is legitimate. This idea, however, belongs to Deuteronomy (Dt. xii., cf. 2 K. xxiii.), up to which period the altars of "the high places" were recognised.

But though the story is late in its present form, it must have had some historical background. The fact that the Western tribes contemplated taking the field against their brethren (*vv.* 12, 33) shows that there was some deep cause of offence, probably (as the story implies) arising from some religious difference.

The half tribe of Manasseh is included with Reuben and Gad throughout the story, with the exception of *vv.* 25, 33, 34. From this it is inferred that the story was originally concerned with Reuben and Gad alone, but that the editor who introduced the half tribe of Manasseh in order to harmonize with the later tradition concerning that tribe (see on xiii. 29) inadvertently omitted to mention it in the verses stated.

9 And the children of Reuben and the children of Gad and the half tribe of Manasseh returned, and departed from the children of Israel out of Shiloh, which is in the land of Canaan, to go unto the land of Gilead, to the land of their possession, whereof they were possessed, according to the commandment of the LORD by the hand 10 of Moses. And when they came unto the region about

---

9. the children of Israel] It is noticeable that throughout the story this expression is restricted to the western tribes, as if the writer held that the eastern tribes had no lot or portion in Israel. In *v.* 19, moreover, the western tribes insinuate that the land of their eastern brethren was not Jehovah's possession. It is still more remarkable that the eastern tribes, in *v.* 22, use **Israel** of the western tribes as opposed to themselves.

Jordan, that is in the land of Canaan, the children of
Reuben and the children of Gad and the half tribe of
Manasseh built there an altar by Jordan, a great altar to
see to. And the children of Israel heard say, Behold, the 11
children of Reuben and the children of Gad and the half
tribe of Manasseh have built an altar in the forefront of
the land of Canaan, in the region about Jordan, on the
side that pertaineth to the children of Israel. And when 12
the children of Israel heard of it, the whole congregation
of the children of Israel gathered themselves together at
Shiloh, to go up against them to war.

*13-20. Phinehas heads a deputation, which presses upon the
trans-Jordanic tribes the danger of their action.*

And the children of Israel sent unto the children of 13
Reuben, and to the children of Gad, and to the half tribe
of Manasseh, into the land of Gilead, Phinehas the son
of Eleazar the priest; and with him ten princes, one 14
prince of a fathers' house for each of the tribes of Israel;
and they were every one of them head of their fathers'
houses among the thousands of Israel. And they came 15
unto the children of Reuben, and to the children of Gad,
and to the half tribe of Manasseh, unto the land of Gilead,
and they spake with them, saying, Thus saith the whole 16
congregation of the LORD, What trespass is this that ye
have committed against the God of Israel, to turn away

---

10. a great altar to see to] i.e. one of imposing dimensions
and which could be seen from a distance.

11. in the forefront of] Rather (as viii. 33, Ex. xxxiv. 3) **in
front of**, i.e. on the border of.

on the side that pertaineth etc.] The altar was on the western
side of Jordan (*v.* 10).

13. Phinehas] The grandson of Aaron (xxiv. 33), and
chiefly remarkable for his righteous zeal at Shittim (Num. xxv.
6-9, Ps. cvi. 30, Ecclus. xlv. 23, 24).

14. a fathers' house] Here it means a tribe (so Num. xvii.
2). Cf. on ii. 12.

this day from following the LORD, in that ye have builded
17 you an altar, to rebel this day against the LORD? Is
the iniquity of Peor too little for us, from which we have
not cleansed ourselves unto this day, although there came
18 a plague upon the congregation of the LORD, that ye
must turn away this day from following the LORD? and
it will be, seeing ye rebel to-day against the LORD, that
to-morrow he will be wroth with the whole congregation
19 of Israel. Howbeit, if the land of your possession be
unclean, then pass ye over unto the land of the possession
of the LORD, wherein the LORD's tabernacle dwelleth,
and take possession among us : but rebel not against the
LORD, nor rebel against us, in building you an altar
20 besides the altar of the LORD our God. Did not Achan
the son of Zerah commit a trespass in the devoted thing,
and wrath fell upon all the congregation of Israel? and
that man perished not alone in his iniquity.

21–29. *The trans-Jordanic tribes exculpate themselves.*

21 Then the children of Reuben and the children of Gad
and the half tribe of Manasseh answered, and spake unto

---

17. Peor] in Num. xxiii. 28 is a mountain. The licentious
worship of the Baal of Peor is also referred to in Num. xxv. 18
and xxxi. 16, and is described in Num. xxv. 1–5. Cf. also Ps.
cvi. 28, Hos. ix. 10. On Beth-peor see xiii. 20.

plague] This word properly means "stroke," and is used for
a divine visitation of any kind (Gen. xii. 17).

19. unclean] i.e. as being a land where Jehovah did not dwell,
or could not dwell on account of idolatry or other iniquity.

the LORD'S tabernacle] The tent of meeting (see on xviii. 1)
was the original sanctuary of the Israelites, and from it later
writers (e.g. Ex. xxv. 8–xxvii. 19) evolved the idea of the
imposing, tent-like structure called the tabernacle. The word
tabernacle means "tent" (Lat. *tabernaculum*).

20. See ch. vii.

and that man etc.] The Heb. is difficult. The following
arrangement of the sentences brings out the meaning more
clearly :—" and did not wrath fall upon all the congregation,
though he was one by himself [i.e. though he was the single
culprit]? did he not die for his guilt?"

the heads of the thousands of Israel, The LORD, the God 22
of gods, the LORD, the God of gods, he knoweth, and
Israel he shall know; if it be in rebellion, or if in trespass
against the LORD, (save thou us not this day,) that we 23
have built us an altar to turn away from following the
LORD; or if to offer thereon burnt offering or meal
offering, or if to offer sacrifices of peace offerings thereon,
let the LORD himself require it; and if we have not *rather* 24
out of carefulness done this, *and* of purpose, saying, In
time to come your children might speak unto our children,
saying, What have ye to do with the LORD, the God of
Israel? for the LORD hath made Jordan a border between 25
us and you, ye children of Reuben and children of Gad;
ye have no portion in the LORD: so shall your children
make our children cease from fearing the LORD. There- 26
fore we said, Let us now prepare to build us an altar,
not for burnt offering, nor for sacrifice: but it shall be a 27
witness between us and you, and between our generations
after us, that we may do the service of the LORD before
him with our burnt offerings, and with our sacrifices, and
with our peace offerings; that your children may not say
to our children in time to come, Ye have no portion in
the LORD. Therefore said we, It shall be, when they so 28
say to us or to our generations in time to come, that we
shall say, Behold the pattern of the altar of the LORD,
which our fathers made, not for burnt offering, nor for
sacrifice; but it is a witness between us and you. God 29
forbid that we should rebel against the LORD, and turn

---

22.   **and Israel** etc.] i.e. Israel, too, shall know.
    save thou etc.] may be a prayer addressed to Jehovah.
24.   **out of carefulness**...and **of purpose**] Lit. "from fear of
something," i.e. from fear of possible consequences (which they
proceed to describe).
27.   **a witness**] Cf. xxiv. 27, Gen. xxxi. 48, Dt. xxxi. 26.
29.   **God forbid**] The Heb. is a solemn form of adjuration
but does not contain the divine name. It is also rendered "far
be it" (Gen. xviii. 25).

away this day from following the LORD, to build an altar
for burnt offering, for meal offering, or for sacrifice,
besides the altar of the LORD our God that is before his
tabernacle.

30–34. *The tribes on the west of Jordan declare themselves satisfied.*

30 And when Phinehas the priest, and the princes of the
congregation, even the heads of the thousands of Israel
which were with him, heard the words that the children
of Reuben and the children of Gad and the children of
31 Manasseh spake, it pleased them well. And Phinehas
the son of Eleazar the priest said unto the children of
Reuben, and to the children of Gad, and to the children
of Manasseh, This day we know that the LORD is in the
midst of us, because ye have not committed this trespass
against the LORD: now have ye delivered the children of
32 Israel out of the hand of the LORD. And Phinehas the
son of Eleazar the priest, and the princes, returned from
the children of Reuben, and from the children of Gad, out
of the land of Gilead, unto the land of Canaan, to the
33 children of Israel, and brought them word again. And
the thing pleased the children of Israel ; and the children
of Israel blessed God, and spake no more of going up
against them to war, to destroy the land wherein the
34 children of Reuben and the children of Gad dwelt. And
the children of Reuben and the children of Gad called
the altar *Ed*: For, *said they*, it is a witness between us
that the LORD is God.

----

34. Ed] marg. " That is, Witness." The name of the altar
has fallen out of the Heb. It was probably some word containing *Ed* (cf. *Galeed*, Gen. xxxi. 47).

xxiii. 1–13. *Joshua in his old age assembles the people and exhorts them against intermingling with the conquered nations of Canaan.*

Ch. xxiii. 2–16 and xxiv. 2–15 contain two farewell addresses by Joshua.   That in ch. xxiii. is later than the address in ch. xxiv. and is strongly Deuteronomic in character (cf. p. viii, note 3).   It may be ascribed to the author of ch. i. and should be compared with that chapter and also with the similar speeches of Moses (e.g. Dt. xxx. 15–xxxi. 8).

And it came to pass after many days, when the LORD **23** had given rest unto Israel from all their enemies round about, and Joshua was old and well stricken in years; that 2 Joshua called for all Israel, for their elders and for their heads, and for their judges and for their officers, and said unto them, I am old and well stricken in years: and ye 3 have seen all that the LORD your God hath done unto all these nations because of you; for the LORD your God, he it is that hath fought for you.   Behold, I have allotted 4 unto you these nations that remain, to be an inheritance for your tribes, from Jordan, with all the nations that I have cut off, even unto the great sea toward the going down of the sun.   And the LORD your God, he shall 5 thrust them out from before you, and drive them from out of your sight; and ye shall possess their land, as the LORD your God spake unto you.   Therefore be ye very 6 courageous to keep and to do all that is written in the book of the law of Moses, that ye turn not aside therefrom to the right hand or to the left; that ye come not 7 among these nations, these that remain among you; neither make mention of the name of their gods, nor cause to swear *by them*, neither serve them, nor bow down yourselves unto them: but cleave unto the LORD 8

---

xxiii. 7.   nor cause to swear by them] i.e. cause oaths to be made in their name.   But a simpler reading is "nor swear by them" (cf. Jer. v. 7, xii. 16, and Dt. vi. 13).

9 your God, as ye have done unto this day. For the LORD
hath driven out from before you great nations and strong :
but as for you, no man hath stood before you unto this
10 day. One man of you shall chase a thousand : for the
LORD your God, he it is that fighteth for you, as he spake
11 unto you. Take good heed therefore unto yourselves,
12 that ye love the LORD your God. Else if ye do in any
wise go back, and cleave unto the remnant of these
nations, even these that remain among you, and make
marriages with them, and go in unto them, and they to
13 you : know for a certainty that the LORD your God will
no more drive these nations from out of your sight ; but
they shall be a snare and a trap unto you, and a scourge
in your sides, and thorns in your eyes, until ye perish
from off this good land which the LORD your God hath
given you.

> 14-16. *He warns the people that as the promises of Jehovah have
> been exactly fulfilled, so will his threatened punishments fall
> on them if they are disobedient.*

14 And, behold, this day I am going the way of all the
earth : and ye know in all your hearts and in all your
souls, that not one thing hath failed of all the good things
which the LORD your God spake concerning you ; all are
come to pass unto you, not one thing hath failed thereof.
15 And it shall come to pass, that as all the good things are
come upon you of which the LORD your God spake unto
you, so shall the LORD bring upon you all the evil things,
until he have destroyed you from off this good land which
16 the LORD your God hath given you. When ye transgress
the covenant of the LORD your God, which he commanded

---

8.   **as ye have done unto this day**]   Contrast xxiv. 14, 23.

12.   **make marriages**]   See Ex. xxxiv. 16, Dt. vii. 3, 1 K.
xi. 2, and Introd. p. x.

14.   **this day**] i.e. presently.

15.   **the evil things**] mentioned in Dt. xxviii. 15-68.

you, and go and serve other gods, and bow down yourselves to them; then shall the anger of the LORD be
kindled against you, and ye shall perish quickly from off
the good land which he hath given unto you.

xxiv. 1–13. *Joshua gathers the people to Shechem and in a
farewell speech summarizes their history.*

And Joshua gathered all the tribes of Israel to Shechem, 24
and called for the elders of Israel, and for their heads,
and for their judges, and for their officers; and they
presented themselves before God. And Joshua said unto 2
all the people, Thus saith the LORD, the God of Israel,
Your fathers dwelt of old time beyond the River, even
Terah, the father of Abraham, and the father of Nahor:
and they served other gods. And I took your father 3
Abraham from beyond the River, and led him throughout
all the land of Canaan, and multiplied his seed, and gave
him Isaac. And I gave unto Isaac Jacob and Esau: 4
and I gave unto Esau mount Seir, to possess it; and
Jacob and his children went down into Egypt. And I 5
sent Moses and Aaron, and I plagued Egypt, according
to that which I did in the midst thereof: and afterward
I brought you out. And I brought your fathers out of 6
Egypt: and ye came unto the sea; and the Egyptians
pursued after your fathers with chariots and with horse-
men unto the Red Sea. And when they cried out unto 7

---

16. other gods] A frequent Deuteronomic expression, but
one that is occasionally found in earlier writers (xxiv. 2, 16, Ex.
xx. 3, xxiii. 13).

xxiv. 1. and they presented themselves before God] Cf.
1 S. x. 19.

2. even Terah...Nahor] A gloss; Terah is the only "father"
mentioned. For the story see Gen. xi. 26–28.

other gods] See on xxiii. 16. For the gods of the patriarchal
age see Gen. xxxi. 19, 30, xxxv. 2, 4, Judith v. 6, 7.

6. the Red Sea] This name has come to us through the
Greek. The Heb. means "sea of reeds."

7. A slight textual change would make this verse read more

the LORD, he put darkness between you and the Egyptians,
and brought the sea upon them, and covered them ; and
your eyes saw what I did in Egypt : and ye dwelt in the
8 wilderness many days.   And I brought you into the land
of the Amorites, which dwelt beyond Jordan ; and they
fought with you : and I gave them into your hand, and
ye possessed their land ; and I destroyed them from
9 before you.   Then Balak the son of Zippor, king of Moab,
arose and fought against Israel ; and he sent and called
10 Balaam the son of Beor to curse you : but I would not
hearken unto Balaam ; therefore he blessed you still : so
11 I delivered you out of his hand.   And ye went over
Jordan, and came unto Jericho : and the men of Jericho
fought against you, the Amorite, and the Perizzite, and
the Canaanite, and the Hittite, and the Girgashite, the
Hivite, and the Jebusite ; and I delivered them into your
12 hand.   And I sent the hornet before you, which drave
them out from before you, even the two kings of the
13 Amorites ; not with thy sword, nor with thy bow.   And I
gave you a land whereon thou hadst not laboured, and
cities which ye built not, and ye dwell therein ; of vine-
yards and oliveyards which ye planted not do ye eat.

---

naturally : " And when ye cried unto me, I put darkness..."
(Ex. xiv. 10, 20).

9.   and fought against Israel] This is not recorded elsewhere.   Cf. Jud. xi. 25.

11.   and the men etc.] This is not explicitly stated in the story
of the capture of Jericho.

12.   the hornet] A figurative expression for the fear (cf. ii.
11, v. 1) that the approach of the Israelites aroused in their
enemies.   So Ex. xxiii. 27, 28, Dt. vii. 20.

the two kings of the Amorites] i.e. Sihon and Og.   But as
the writer is now dealing with the conquests *west* of the Jordan,
the mention of these eastern kings is out of place.   The words
are probably a gloss.

13. Cf. xi. 13 and Dt. vi. 10, 11.

14, 15. He exhorts the people to serve Jehovah.

Now therefore fear the LORD, and serve him in sincerity 14
and in truth : and put away the gods which your fathers
served beyond the River, and in Egypt ; and serve ye the
LORD.   And if it seem evil unto you to serve the LORD, 15
choose you this day whom ye will serve ; whether the
gods which your fathers served that were beyond the
River, or the gods of the Amorites, in whose land ye
dwell : but as for me and my house, we will serve the
LORD.

*16-24. His exhortation meets with a favourable and
immediate response.*

And the people answered and said, God forbid that 16
we should forsake the LORD, to serve other gods ; for 17
the LORD our God, he it is that brought us and our
fathers up out of the land of Egypt, from the house of
bondage, and that did those great signs in our sight, and
preserved us in all the way wherein we went, and among .
all the peoples through the midst of whom we passed : and 18
the LORD drave out from before us all the peoples, even
the Amorites which dwelt in the land : therefore we also
will serve the LORD ; for he is our God.   And Joshua 19
said unto the people, Ye cannot serve the LORD ; for he
is an holy God ; he is a jealous God ; he will not forgive

---

14.   serve him in sincerity and in truth]   The original for
sincerity implies "completeness."

and put away the gods etc.]   So *v*. 23.   The writer implies,
in contradiction to xxiii. 8, that the worship of strange gods was
general amongst the Israelites in Joshua's day.   As he says
nothing of its illegality on the ground of its contravening earlier
commands to worship Jehovah only, it seems as if in his view
such earlier commands had not been given.   Gods of the Habiru
are mentioned in cuneiform inscriptions found in Ḥatti (Introd.
p. xiv).

and in Egypt]   Cf. Ezek. xx. 5-9, Amos v. 25, 26.

15.   the gods of the Amorites etc.]   See Introd. p. xviii.

19.   jealous was originally another form of "zealous"

20 your transgression nor your sins.   If ye forsake the
LORD, and serve strange gods, then he will turn and do
you evil, and consume you, after that he hath done you
21 good.   And the people said unto Joshua, Nay ; but we
22 will serve the LORD.   And Joshua said unto the people,
Ye are witnesses against yourselves that ye have chosen
you the LORD, to serve him.   And they said, We are
23 witnesses.   Now therefore put away, *said he*, the strange
gods which are among you, and incline your heart unto
24 the LORD, the God of Israel.   And the people said unto
Joshua, The LORD our God will we serve, and unto his
voice will we hearken.

25-28.   *A covenant is made and attested by the erection*
of a stone.

25 So Joshua made a covenant with the people that day,
and set them a statute and an ordinance in Shechem.
26   And Joshua wrote these words in the book of the law
of God ; and he took a great stone, and set it up there
under the oak that was by the sanctuary of the LORD.
27 And Joshua said unto all the people, Behold, this stone
shall be a witness against us ; for it hath heard all the
words of the LORD which he spake unto us : it shall be
therefore a witness against you, lest ye deny your God.

(=" ardent, anxious ") and came to mean " angry at any rivalry
or interference."; cf. Nahum i. 2, Zech. viii. 2, and for the
meaning, Is. xlii. 8 (" my glory will I not give to another ").
   20. strange gods] So *v.* 23.   That is, gods of foreign
peoples (whether the gods of Haran or of Canaan, *v.* 15).
   25. set them etc.] i.e. set before them the terms of the
covenant.   Cf. Ex. xv. 25, 26.
   26.   The writing in the book of the law of God is a later
Deuteronomic comment on the setting up of the stone.   Cf. i. 8,
viii. 30–32, Dt. xxxi. 9, 24.
   these words] i.e. apparently a statement of the events just
recorded.
   27. it hath heard]   The deity resident in the stone was cog-
nizant of what had taken place.   Cf. Gen. xxxi. 52.

So Joshua sent the people away, every man unto his 28
inheritance.

29–33. *Concluding notices*

And it came to pass after these things, that Joshua the 29
son of Nun, the servant of the LORD, died, being an
hundred and ten years old. And they buried him in the 30
border of his inheritance in Timnath-serah, which is in
the hill country of Ephraim, on the north of the mountain
of Gaash. And Israel served the LORD all the days of 31
Joshua, and all the days of the elders that outlived Joshua,
and had known all the work of the LORD, that he had
wrought for Israel. And the bones of Joseph, which the 32
children of Israel brought up out of Egypt, buried they
in Shechem, in the parcel of ground which Jacob bought
of the sons of Hamor the father of Shechem for an
hundred pieces of money: and they became the inheritance of the children of Joseph. And Eleazar the 33
son of Aaron died; and they buried him in the hill of
Phinehas his son, which was given him in the hill country
of Ephraim.

---

28. Cf. Jud. ii. 6.

29–31. Cf. Jud. ii. 7–9.

32. the bones of Joseph] See Gen. l. 24–26, Ex. xiii. 19,
Heb. xi. 22.

parcel] from Lat. *particula* = "small part." Ruth iv. 3, John
iv. 5.

which Jacob bought] See Gen. xxxiii. 19.

pieces of money] Heb. *ḳesiṭah*. The weight of the *ḳesiṭah*,
mentioned only here, Gen. xxxiii. 19 and Job xlii. 11, is not
known.

they became] i.e. either the bones of Joseph, or Shechem and
the parcel of ground.

33. the hill of Phinehas] = (as marg.) *Gibeah of Phinehas*;
cf. *Gibeath-ha-araloth* (v. 3), and *Gibeah of Saul* (1 S. xi. 4).

The burial of Eleazar in a place that was named after his son
is strange enough to warrant the suggestion that this verse originally recorded the death and burial of Phinehas.

INDEX

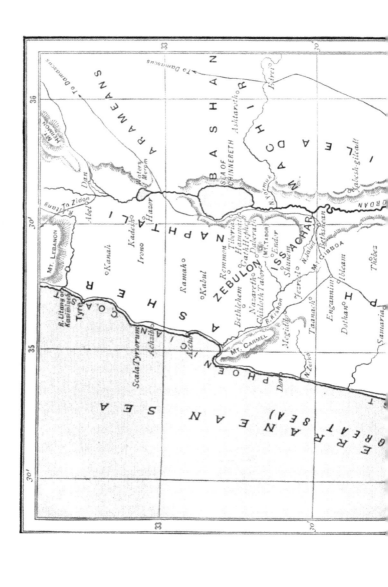

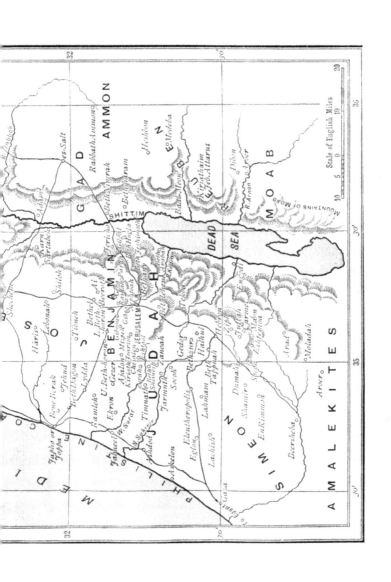

For EU product safety concerns, contact us at Calle de José Abascal, 56–1°, 28003 Madrid, Spain or eugpsr@cambridge.org.

www.ingramcontent.com/pod-product-compliance
Ingram Content Group UK Ltd.
Pitfield, Milton Keynes, MK11 3LW, UK
UKHW020311140625
459647UK00018B/1827